MW00398049

Blue Days, Black Nights

Blue Days, Black Nights

a memoir

RON NYSWANER

Advocate BOOKS

MANUFACTURED IN THE UNITED STATES OF AMERICA.

THIS TRADE PAPERBACK ORIGINAL IS PUBLISHED BY ALYSON PUBLICATIONS,
P.O. BOX 4371, LOS ANGELES, CALIFORNIA 90078-4371.
DISTRIBUTION IN THE UNITED KINGDOM BY
    TURNAROUND PUBLISHER SERVICES LTD.,
UNIT 3, OLYMPIA TRADING ESTATE, COBURG ROAD, WOOD GREEN,
LONDON N22 6TZ ENGLAND.

FIRST EDITION: OCTOBER 2004

04 05 06 07 08 ■ 10 9 8 7 6 5 4 3 2 1

ISBN 1-55583-889-8

LIBRARY OF CONGRESS CATALOGING-IN-PUBLICATION DATA
  NYSWANER, RON.
    BLUE DAYS, BLACK NIGHTS : A MEMOIR / RON NYSWANER.—1ST ED.
    ISBN 1-55583-889-8
    1. NYSWANER, RON. 2. LOS ANGELES (CALIF.)—SOCIAL LIFE AND CUSTOMS.
    3. MALE PROSTITUTES—CALIFORNIA—LOS ANGELES. 4. NARCOTIC HABIT—
    CALIFORNIA—LOS ANGELES. 5. SCREENWRITERS—UNITED STATES—
    BIOGRAPHY. 6. GAY MEN—UNITED STATES—BIOGRAPHY. I. TITLE.
  PS3564.Y775Z463 2004
  818'.5403—DC22
  [B]   2004052480

CREDITS
FRONT JACKET PHOTOGRAPHY BY ALAN THORNTON/STONE COLLECTION.
JACKET DESIGN BY MATT SAMS.

For Johann, who walked me through the darkness.

And for James, who welcomed me into the light.

Prologue

The grave digger struck the frozen snow with his shovel, making a hopeless-sounding thud, unable to penetrate more than an inch or two. When I urged him, with mimed gestures and grunts, to keep digging, he crossed his arms, balancing the shovel against his elbow, and fixed a look on me that managed to convey contempt and pity at the same time. I recognized this expression, having seen it recently on the faces of police, undertakers, emergency room nurses, priests, and psychiatrists. The grave digger's colleagues, with their own useless shovels, joined their leader for a socialist-style work stoppage. Before I could protest through my intrepid translator, two of the grave diggers answered their cell phones. All the Hungarians, including my companions, responded to this interruption by lighting cigarettes.

I had traveled to the northern region of Hungary, near the Slovak border, to arrange a funeral, but the preparations had been hampered by a snap of icy weather. My translator—a girl of twenty named Kitty, from the nearest village—explained that the grave diggers would have to build a fire over the grave site, dig a few inches of reluctant earth, start a new fire, and dig again, repeating the operation until they'd reached the appropriate depth. They had halted work to renegotiate their fee to cover the extra time and effort.

"Give them anything they want," I said.

Kitty flicked her hand in my direction, urging me to be quiet, placing herself protectively between me and the others.

1

The leader of the grave diggers finished his phone call, and he and Kitty began to argue, the breath of each—turned white by cold air and cigarette smoke—merging into a single cloud. I walked a few steps, turned my back, dug a Vicodin out of my pocket, and swallowed it without anything to wash it down.

The casket holding Johann waited in the funeral chapel, near the entrance to the cemetery; I could glimpse it through a cracked window. Johann's brother and cousin walked past me to join the discussion between Kitty and the grave diggers. I was happy to stand alone, to gaze at Johann's casket, to remain aloof from the negotiations, comforted by the impenetrable language of Hungarian the way one is comforted by the murmur of a conversation in the neighboring apartment, serving as a sign of life but mercifully indistinct and anonymous. At least, while they were arguing, no one asked how Johann had died or suggested I elaborate on my improvised lies. The grave diggers' strike had rescued me, for the time being, from explanation.

I couldn't tell Johann's family the truth about his final hours, our bitter words to each other, his splenetic accusations and my feeble defenses. I couldn't speak of the circumstances under which we had met nor give details of Johann's American career. I was incapable of describing our relationship—professional, intimate, confounding, sporadic—and relied on the singular, inadequate "friend." I couldn't imagine trying to describe Johann's life in the United States to his perplexed, grieving relatives through Kitty with her university-stiff grammar, detailing the seedy, Hollywood apartments, his felonious cronies, or his contempt for the lonely men who pursued and desired him.

I couldn't explain—to anyone, including myself—how I had come to this place in my life where I sought, nearly exclusively, the company of outlaw lovers like Johann, men who sold themselves by the hour. I couldn't comprehend my own life. Or two lives, rather, for I had managed to maintain a presence in the respectable, daylight world (screenwriting assignments, volunteer work, tending ill parents, gardening) while making forays to darker places, like a superhero gone bad, who changes costume when the sun sets and commits crimes by moonlight. At least—and this was a comfort—Johann and I had fun.

Certainly, I couldn't tell anyone about the wounds on my chest, where—hours after Johann died—I had carved his initials into my skin with a serrated knife. The wounds had scabbed over, and I fell asleep—in my chilly room at the local inn, the Hotel Bodrog—caressing the carvings as if caressing Johann. It was Johann's final joke that I had carved the wrong initials into my chest, since he had lied to me about his name. I didn't discover his true name until I started making funeral arrangements, after I had tattooed myself.

I turned back to the grave site. Kitty was making a passionate speech, pointing to me, to Johann's casket, to his brother, and to the pocked snow where Johann's grave was to be dug. The grave diggers looked shamed and solemn, clasping felt hats in red, callused hands and deflecting their eyes to the snow. Their faces were jowly, blotched pink and white, their bodies squat and strong. They reminded me of men from my childhood home (southwestern Pennsylvania, bituminous coal mining country): Poles and Czechs, and Hungarians who were called "Hunkies," noted for raucous weddings and plaster statues of the Virgin Mary on their front lawns. Where I was born, a good Hunky wedding ended in a brawl and required the intervention of state troopers.

For three days I had lived in Johann's village while arranging his funeral. I know I was a strange sight: a bleary-eyed, sometimes weeping American buying up all the town's candles and flowers, pale blue tapers with a soapy feel and salmon-colored gladiolas. But I was consoled by the people of Johann's hometown, their round faces and simple houses, the dinner plates filled with noodles and gravy. How odd that Johann should take me—as the final stop on our tour—to a place that felt so familiar.

3

Suddenly, everyone was laughing, indicating détente had been reached. Kitty took a wad of red and blue forints from my hand and passed them around, prompting vigorous hand-shaking and double-cheek kissing. I followed Kitty to our car to continue with the day's scheduled events: ordering flowers and a headstone, and arranging a funeral mass.

As we plodded past the chapel, I glanced again at Johann's casket; it was shining, silver, and oddly rounded at the ends, like a capsule. I felt wet snow sopping my boots and thought of a time in Key West when Johann had thrown miniature fire-crackers at my feet. When I jumped, shrieking, he planted his hands on his hips and belly-laughed. I crooked my arm around his neck, a mock wrestling pose, and we clung to each other, oblivious to the stares of the sunburned passersby. That afternoon he bought me a present, the first he'd ever given, a T-shirt with a prophetic message on the back: "If you're not living on the edge, you're taking up too much space."

Rock

One

I met Johann in a bar called Numbers on Sunset Boulevard two blocks east of the Chateau Marmont Hotel.

I spotted him as he walked down the stairs, from the upper-level entrance, in black storm trooper boots, a leather jacket, and jeans bearing a European logo. With his blond hair thinning and slicked back, gelled to a shimmering veneer; pale cheeks; and thin, colorless lips, he was no one's idea of a pretty boy. But his bearing caught and held my attention. His shoulders were broad above a taut waist, back straight as a fence post, arms bent at his belt: a boxer coming out of his corner after the bell has rung. He focused a withering glare on bystanders crossing his path, paunchy customers, lanky hustlers (the eponymous "numbers"), taking them in, sizing them up, sizing *me* up, when his high-beam eyes met mine but continued, too soon, scouring the room. Other eyes tried to catch his attention and failed as he fished for prospects but offered no encouragement. He planted himself in a pool of track lighting, hands on his hips, expecting to be approached, like fearsome royalty willing to consider petitions for mercy.

I was stuck at the bar entertaining a tall, befuddled, possibly stoned young man named Gordon who was telling me about his acting class, a scene study, in which he was preparing the part of, as he put it, "Anthony Hopkins in *The Silence of the Lambs.*"

I looked past my tall companion's biceps as a nervous, overweight tourist approached the storm trooper with tentative jabs at conversation. I had a sinking feeling I had missed an opportunity. Hope rose as the heavy out-of-towner—wearing a tragically all-wrong kelly green sweater—guffawed at his own joke, and the storm trooper turned his face away, as if offended by the man's breath. My tall friend droned on, delivering one of Hannibal Lecter's monologues in a voice that seemed to come from the ceiling, disembodied and celestial: *"Are the lambs still screaming, Clarice?"*

I kept my eyes on my blond demigod, who shoved his hands into his pockets and turned down—with a barely perceptible shake of his head, really a tiny jerk of the chin—an offer of a drink from the tourist.

"I ate his kidney with some fava beans and a nice chi-an-ti."

My drink arrived and I sucked gin from the olives, plotting to engage the storm trooper. I was no better at this than the unlucky man in kelly green. I fumbled words and made literary references that shot over the heads of my intended conquests. Fearing rejection, I spoke too bluntly and too soon of my sundry accomplishments. My appearance confused the young men. I wasn't as old as most of the customers. I didn't wear my wealth in an obvious manner, with Italian jackets and Rolex watches. I possessed a careless—some might say, incoherent—sense of style: Kenneth Cole shoes and a Fossil watch, a Wilke-Rodriguez jacket over a Gap T-shirt, tattoos and earrings and metal-framed eyeglasses with bifocal lenses. On good days I thought of myself as eclectic. But that night, in Numbers, facing those men who belonged comfortably and wholeheartedly to a *category*—buyers and sellers, appropriately costumed—I felt muddled and out of place. I was drawn to the storm trooper's confidence, his sense of self. Here was a young man who would never—one can just sense these things—waste time with an acting class.

"Anthony Hopkins is the *actor*," I said. Gordon was so tall I found myself lecturing his armpit. "Hannibal Lecter is the *character*. When you act, you play a character."

Gordon's mouth hung open, as if my criticism had smacked him in the face. I backtracked to soften the blow. "But you're doing the right thing. You're studying. You're taking the craft seriously. That's the first step." I threw ten dollars onto the bar. "Buy yourself a drink."

I meandered toward the blond, planting myself into the glare of his headlights, attempting a look of nonchalance, sucking on the toothpick that had skewered the olives of my martini. Unfortunately, the toothpick tumbled from my lips and clung, almost magically, to my lapel, sticking out like a miniature crinkled wooden erection. All the while, my storm trooper beheld me with his flinty, blue-gray eyes, with barely a discernible expression on his features, only boredom beneath a patina of pity.

He spoke. "Hello."

"Hello." He did not take his eyes from mine. What to say? "I was drinking a martini. I like them for the olives. It's my favorite vegetable."

No reply. I was stuck, speechless, beginning to perspire. I remembered the confidence I had manage to project at lunch, earlier in the day, with a producer, a director, and two film executives. I had no problem speaking then; in fact, I held court for several minutes, recounting my trip to the Yucatán over the Christmas holiday, how I rolled my rental car down a gully, flipping it three times, coming to a stop upside down, with the car smashed like an accordion and my luggage strewn about the jungle while vultures circled overhead. I'd caught a ride to Mérida, where hours later I was tossed out of a bar for kissing a bullfighter named Flavio, after purchasing for Flavio and his fourteen comrades, all of whom claimed to be bullfighters, nine rounds of flaming tequila drinks sucked through a frozen straw. The anecdote had been a triumph in the film studio's commissary, when I used it to cut short a discussion of day care. I considered recounting my Mexican adventure to the storm trooper, demonstrating I had a wild side, despite my metal-framed eyeglasses. *I will buy him a flaming tequila drink and share the frozen straw.*

"I bet you drink tequila."

"I don't drink alcohol," he replied in a Schwarzenegger accent.

Bingo! He is a storm trooper. I'd met one in Vienna twelve years earlier. A paratrooper named Rolf in a bar called Why Not? But Rolf had no trouble making conversation.

I caught sight of Gordon smiling at me from above the heads of all the smoking, drinking, chatting customers. In the blaze of my storm trooper's studied indifference, my vacated stool seemed a haven, even if it meant spending the rest of the evening eye to nipple with Gordon.

"Well…" I turned a shoulder toward the bar.

"But I wouldn't mind a Diet Pepsi."

We found a table where someone had arranged rose petals floating in a tiny bowl of water. I wondered if the romantic gesture was wasted on the prostitutes and porn stars in the room. My storm trooper lifted a damp rose petal with the tip of his finger and told me a few things about himself, speaking in a low, accented voice, like an actor in a B movie about the Nazis. His name was Johann. He was German, a student at USC, majoring in international business; he hoped to run his own import-export company. He spoke five languages, including Latin.

"Say something in Latin."

Johann roasted a rose petal in the flame of a candle and grunted, "Quid pro quo."

I told him I was a writer. I waited for the typical questions and anticipated providing self-aggrandizing answers: What do you write? Screenplays. Anything I've ever heard of? This was the climactic point, at which I would reveal my minor-celebrity status as the author of *Philadelphia.* I had found in the years following the film's release that my brush with fame conferred something on me that impressed people, and the content of the film—its strengths, its weaknesses, and the controversy surrounding it— faded in the light of its success. People had heard of the film, read about it, seen it, or rented it, or at least knew people who had seen it or rented it. Broaching the subject with a rehearsed modesty, declaring I was a "writer," and allowing the conversation to take its usual course, led—in most cases—to congratulations, a hand-shake, a "wow," or a request for an autograph.

When I told Johann I was a writer, he said, "Maybe you should write the story of my life."

It was time to take the plunge. "Do you think we might be able to spend some time together tonight?"

"My rate is one hundred and fifty dollars an hour."

"You have underpriced yourself."

Johann laughed—a real, tossing-his-head-back laugh. When I raised my arm for the waiter, he brought it to my side, our first moment of physical contact.

"We don't have time for that," he said. "Aren't you anxious to get going?"

But I wasn't ready. The martini hadn't done its job; my neck felt stiff and my hands were ice. "I need something," I whispered.

It was a relief when he smiled. "I'll call someone."

"You don't mind?"

"I don't do drugs myself. But for clients, I know how to get them."

Ten minutes later I was backing out of the parking lot. Johann sat beside me, jamming his storm trooper boots against the dashboard. He shook off my suggestion to use the seat belt. When I reminded him he was breaking the law, he snorted, "I thought America was a free country." He strapped himself in and sank into a black mood. "My friend is not home," he said. "I have no drugs for you. By the way, *they* are against the law too."

Suddenly the Filipino parking valet was running toward us, waving his arms and shouting in his native tongue. I panicked. Had he overheard Johann's comment about drugs? "What is he saying?" I asked. Johann shrugged. Apparently, Tagalog was not one of his five languages. I kept the car sliding backward, hoping to escape. But the tiny, brown-skinned valet threw himself onto the hood.

Johann gripped my leg. "Ronnie, stop."

I obeyed and the Filipino attendant's head clunked against the windshield. Johann gestured for me to look out the window toward the rear of the car. I saw a line of metal teeth across the parking lot entrance and one of those signs that prepares you for SEVERE TIRE DAMAGE. The valet had been trying to warn me.

"I'm sorry!" I shouted. I started the car toward the clearly designated exit, tossing a twenty out the window. Johann laughed so hard he gripped his sides.

"Oh, Ronnie! Ronnie! You are crazy!" Johann squeezed my leg harder. Aroused, I turned the wrong way onto a one-way street. Johann unsnapped his seat belt. "I don't think we worry about breaking the law tonight! I will get you drugs, no problem! Maybe I will do some too. Go down to Santa Monica Boulevard," he commanded, referring to the famous avenue that is ground zero for street hustlers. "I'm sure you know where *that* is."

We cruised Fairfax toward Santa Monica, where prostitutes in cutoffs and tank shirts cluster at bus stops and fast-food joints. Johann dismissed them: "Trash. Drug addicts. They let a man fuck them without a condom for fifty bucks. Idiots. No future. No brains. No class. Keep driving east, Ronnie. I am looking for a friend who will get us drugs. He is German too. His name is Fred. I think he got out of jail last week."

I ventured a personal question: "How long have you been doing this?"

"What?"

"Well, you know... Your work. Being a, um..."

Johann rapped his knuckles against the molded plastic dashboard. "Ronnie. I don't think you are very important if they give you such a lousy car."

Before I could defend myself, Johann spotted his drug-dealing friend. "Pull over—that's Fred. The one on crutches."

With Fred and his crutches in the back, we followed his directions toward Hollywood Boulevard. Fred was a scrawny kid with frizzy hair under a red bandanna, wearing a sleeveless T-shirt with the American flag. He looked as if he were going to a costume party as a 1970s heroin addict. "Yeah, yeah, I can get you powder," he said, in an accent thicker than Johann's.

Johann made introductions. "Fred, this is Ronnie. He is a terrible driver. You will probably die tonight. I hope you have made a confession recently."

"I never confess to anything!" Fred proclaimed. "I take my secrets to the grave. I just got out of jail. You know what happens in jail to people who confess? They get their hearts cut out with a shiv."

Johann rolled his eyes. "Fred. It was a joke. Ronnie, turn right at the corner. But first, stop at the red light. Good boy." I wondered if Johann spoke to everyone as if they were retarded children.

Fred directed us through the traffic of Hollywood Boulevard to a side street and a group of young black men lingering outside the Starview Hotel, which offered rooms with three adult channels.

"Give me some money, Ronnie." I handed over two hundred dollars. Johann returned half. "Too much."

"But I want to make sure we get enough."

Johann held firm. "I have school tomorrow. I am sure you have to work. Let Johann take care of you tonight, okay?" He put one hundred dollars into Fred's bony hand. "One gram, Fred."

Fred leaned close. "Listen. These are Crips. I can do business with them. I joined their gang in jail."

Johann was delighted. "Oh, yes, I am sure you are a Crip, Fred. You are a big Crip. You are the president of the Crips, I believe."

Fred spoke gravely. "They don't know me as Fred. I have a gang name. They call me Gestapo." Johann put his hand over his heart as he laughed. Fred continued, "*You* must call me Gestapo."

"No, I am sorry," Johann said. "I must call you Fred. Go do business, Fred. Don't cheat me, Fred, or I will kill you, Fred. Goodbye, Fred."

Johann shut the door and Fred hobbled away.

Two

Beauty is also a gift of God, one of the most rare and precious, and we should be thankful if we are happy enough to possess it and thankful, if we are not, that others possess it for our pleasure.

—W. SOMERSET MAUGHAM, *THE PAINTED VEIL*

We were alone and I was stone cold sober. Gestapo disappeared with the crack dealers. There was a liquor store across the street from which egregiously thin locals emerged carrying pint-size brown bags. One of them puked into a trash can.

The next day's appointments stretched ahead of me: a morning notes session with studio executives for a romantic comedy set in Appalachia and, after lunch, a meeting to pitch an adaptation of a W. Somerset Maugham novel. The Maugham book had been filmed in 1934 with Greta Garbo. It was a romantic epic with a spiritual twist: A couple finds love in the midst of a cholera epidemic. I was prepared to describe the theme of my proposed adaptation as "the grace that comes with unconditional love." I considered rehearsing my pitch on Johann, who was inspecting his fingernails in the dim light.

"You nervous, Ronnie?" Johann pointed to my hands wringing the steering wheel.

"I have appointments tomorrow. I'm in the movie business."

Johann came alive. "Do you know any stars?"

"As a matter of fact, I do."

"Do you know Veronica Azul? She has tits like this." He

15

held his hands around imaginary breasts the size of basket-balls. "Solid plastic. Sometimes I buy coke from her. She wants me to make a movie with her, but I don't think my dick is big enough."

Before I could explain that I worked in the real movie business, not porn, Johann patted my leg. "Don't worry, Ronnie. My dick is not small. You will get your money's worth. Veronica says I have a good look for the movies. Tough. She wants me to do a cop scene with her. She drives and I pull her over. I am dressed like LAPD. I give her a ticket and make her blow me in the car."

"Do you prefer women?"

"Only their breasts." He yawned and checked his pager. "Agh!" he shouted, pointing to the flashing number. "This guy always does this! Punches in his number and then 911. He is so *anxious* for me. He will *die* if I do not call him back *immediately*. 911. 911." He addressed the pager directly. "Relax, my friend. You will not die if you do not hear from Johann for one hour."

"An hour? We haven't gotten home yet. Are you leaving in an hour?"

"Ronnie. Why do you worry?" Johann dropped his voice to a growl. "Tonight *you* are the priority."

The door opened and Gestapo flopped into the backseat. He opened his palm to reveal several orange-yellow pellets that resembled clumps of soap.

"No powder," he announced. "Rock. You have a pipe?"

Finding a crack pipe in Hollywood at one A.M. is not as easy as you might think. Johann, Gestapo, and I drove past bands of hip-hop kids on street corners who appeared, to me, capable of providing assistance, but Gestapo dismissed each group with two words: "Not Crips." He was willing to do business only with Crips. Apparently, every young man on the boulevards of Hollywood this particular evening belonged to the Bloods, mortal enemies of Crips. Gestapo declared that a Crip, such as himself, approaching a Blood to buy a crack pipe would suffer a grave penalty. "They will cut my heart out with a shiv."

What about the Crips who sold us the crack? No, we couldn't go back to them. "What will they think of me? I buy crack, but I don't have a pipe to smoke it? They will think I am stupid. They will cut my heart out with a shiv."

Obviously, Gestapo had acquired a favorite English expression. For as long as I knew Johann, we made each other laugh by summoning this phrase. In a Key West restaurant, brandishing a steak knife, Johann declared, "Ronnie, I will cut your heart out with a shiv." Once, during sex in a New York hotel, I muttered the phrase as best I could while lowering my mouth onto him: "I …ill …ut y…r …art ou… wi… uh …iv."

Johann took charge, swiveling in his seat and getting right into Gestapo's face. "Get me a pipe, Fred. Or I shove this shit"—the crack—"up your ass."

"Throw it out the window!" The suggestion came from me, prompted by exhaustion and something else: a fantasy that Johann could elicit my love sans chemical assistance. My use of drugs and paid-for sex had developed in recent months; one fueled the other, and both seemed to be growing beyond my control. It was a time when I ought to have been happy and satisfied, and yet I was lonely, restless, and anxious. I imagined a therapist might help me understand this contradiction, but I had been raised by stoic parents who abhorred self-examination. I looked for solutions in romance and chance meetings. A new life might begin in this car, on Hollywood Boulevard, with a hustler throwing precious drugs out a window, acting on my impromptu command. Johann might rescue me.

My companions fell quiet. People who abuse drugs do not throw them out a window.

But Johann surprised me. He rolled down the window.

Earlier he had declared his indifference to drugs; perhaps he was about to prove it. I felt a cold sweat cover the top of my head as I waited for him to act. But Johann, who struck me as someone who never hesitated, hesitated. I glimpsed Gestapo in the rearview mirror, his eyes fixed on Johann's clutched hand, his mouth slightly open. We drifted down the street in silence, as if we had passed the scene of an accident and spotted bodies lying on the road. Everything seemed grim and hopeless. Finally, Gestapo spoke, chastened and eager to please. "I will show you how to *make* a pipe!"

Johann closed the window. I turned on the radio and breathed again. I wasn't ready to be rescued.

To make a crack pipe we needed a soda can and steel wool. The soda can was acquired in a Mobil station, where Gestapo treated me and Johann to bubble gum. The steel wool posed a problem. I carried a box of Brillo pads to the counter. Gestapo tossed it at me and snapped, "What do you think we are going to do? Clean the bathtub?"

Johann explained in a whisper, "The soap, Ronnie. Not good for smoking."

The search for soapless steel wool was a bizarre twist on the traditional Hollywood tour, led by Gestapo, from a gas station to a deli to a porn shop, wherever crackheads were likely to seek supplies. Johann leaned back and opened his legs, directing my hand to his inner thigh. I steered the rented car with my free hand. Two hours had passed since meeting Johann; I was in for three hundred dollars at this point. I opened the window and let the Los Angeles air waft over me, smelling of hibiscus and gasoline.

The steel wool was procured in a liquor store, where the proprietor kept a wad of it under the counter, selling stringy chunks for a couple of bucks. Gestapo explained the construction of the pipe, and we delivered him to the Fatburger restaurant on Santa Monica, with a tip of fifty dollars and three rocks of crack.

The drive to my agent's house in Beverly Hills was quiet. Johann closed his eyes and hummed. After a few bars, I recognized the song: "Happy Birthday."

"Is it your birthday?"

"No. It's the only song I know how to sing."

Three

STONE
Dominant Master
6'4", 230 lbs.
Dominant Verbal Top into all aspects
of Safe Dominant Fantasies.
Water Sports, Boxing, Martial Arts,
Wrestling Scenes, 24/7.

—CLASSIFIED "MODEL" ADVERTISEMENT

Johann placed his lips over the opening of the soda can, gesturing for me to light the crack, which nested in steel wool over a second hole freshly punctured with my manicure scissors. The rock sizzled in the flame, and Johann drew a deep breath; the smoke that escaped his lips smelled like singed hair. His facility with the crack belied his claim made earlier in the evening that he didn't do drugs, but I decided to let the discrepancy pass without comment. I was anxious for my turn at the improvised aluminum crack pipe, and had no wish to start an argument with the storm trooper who was holding it.

Whenever I traveled to Los Angeles, I lived in the guest wing of my agent's house, purchased from the estate of Vincent Price. Years ago, someone had painted every room a deep orange. "Coral," my agent explained, "for Vincent's wife, Coral Browne." The walls had been painted over, but my agent kept the original color inside the guest room closet, enjoying the effect on guests when he flung open the closet door and announced, "Imagine every wall of this house in *that* color! *Every wall!*"

Johann's eyes were closed after he inhaled the crack; he sat composed, as if meditating. I wanted his attention, so I opened the closet door and proclaimed, "Imagine every wall in this house painted *that* color!"

"You." He offered the can.

This was new for me. I had snorted my share of cocaine, but smoking crack seemed different, tawdry, and desperate, conjuring TV news images of ravaged urban neighborhoods and bullet-ridden victims of gang wars. I supported a foster home in the Bronx for orphans of crack addicts; I pictured the wide, frightened eyes of the babies on the brochure.

"Sure," I said, swallowing a familiar feeling of disgust.

Johann arranged a waxy rock of crack in the metal nest and placed the can against my lips. He held the lighter and commanded me to inhale. I obeyed. As my body left the ground I heard him say, "Very good, Ronnie. Someday you will be a professional crackhead."

He removed his shirt and took a bodybuilder's stance in front of a mirror. "Not bad, hey, Ronnie?" His torso was muscled, nearly hairless, freckled along the shoulders. His biceps protruded like baseballs. "I go to Sports Connection gym four times a week. I never pay. I run to the place, I get all sweaty. I don't carry a bag. I walk past the desk, no problem. So, Ronnie, you could say I have a free lifetime membership to Sports Connection."

He sat on the edge of the bed and spread his knees. The pose seemed staged, professional. I knew my role; I fell between his legs and opened his pants. Pulling down his jeans, I wondered if *all* the gestures of the evening had been part of a performance: the quips, the accent, placing his hand on my thigh. Was he keeping me on the hook with hopes for a generous tip, running out the meter, like a New York cabbie delivering a tourist from midtown to the Village via the Brooklyn Bridge?

Johann wore no underwear, and his crotch smelled of cologne; I imagined him dabbing himself as he dressed for work. He made no sound as I stroked his pale, lightly haired legs. He looked past me. I followed his gaze to a mirror and caught him staring at our reflection.

I became lost in the feel of him inside my mouth and the salty, sour taste on my tongue. I began to hallucinate. The floor and the ceiling of the room stretched away; we hurtled through the atmosphere in a spaceship deriving its power from the movement of my head bobbing up and down. I heard the Scottish guy from *Star Trek* calling from the engine room, demanding "More power!" and I moved my head faster. The ceiling disappeared and the floor fell away. I held tight to Johann's legs. I had no idea what he was doing above me; I lost awareness of anything above his waist and below his knees. I was afraid to look up, in case Johann's upper half had disappeared. Then, as if I'd been thrown into a tub of cold water, the hallucination vanished. I felt Johann's boots poke my legs and my knees burn against the scratchy carpet.

Johann offered a compliment. "You know what you are doing."

"I've been schooled by professionals."

He settled onto the pillows, arms above his head. "This crack is not so good. I will give Fred a hard time."

I curled against him. "You can always cut his heart out with a shiv."

Johann hummed a few measures of "Happy Birthday." "This is relaxing," he sighed, and began to tell me of his career at the "office," his name for Numbers.

"Usually they hire me as a master. I order them around. I beat them. It makes me tired. I wear a leather mask. It gets sweaty. The next day my face is dry and full of pimples."

I remembered the shame I felt after my own tentative excursions into domination: a spanking on my birthday by a prostitute named Rex; a dog collar placed around my neck by a bodybuilding porn star who asked me to lick his feet, which turned out to be, mercifully, spotless and professionally pedicured ("I take care of my feet," he claimed, in response to a compliment). These episodes had left me bewildered; I didn't understand the pleasure I derived from being subjugated.

"It feels good for these people to let go, to lose control," I ventured, keeping the conversation at a general level, in case Johann viewed his submissive clients with contempt.

"No, Ronnie. These people are lonely."

"How does getting beaten make you feel less lonely?"

Johann shrugged. "Some things happen to these people when they are children. Someone beats them, and they think, *Oh, this is great, this is love.* So I beat them, and they think they get more love. In my profession you cannot be judgmental." Johann turned toward me. "Ronnie? You want me to be the master with *you?*" He posed the question with a complete lack of investment in the answer, the way a waiter inquires if you'd like regular or decaf.

"I'm perfectly satisfied with what we're doing right now." It was true. I liked this man, this nonjudgmental storm trooper, who was slightly above it all yet touched by the complexities and loneliness of his clients. I didn't want him to disappear into some role. And I wasn't afraid of him or nervous about my body or self-conscious; in the light of Johann's aura, I had no need to disappear. I ran a hand along the inside of his thigh, the gesture of a lover, not a slave or a trick or a john.

"Ah, I see. Gentle type, likes to cuddle," he said, placing me in the appropriate category in his mental Rolodex.

Johann described his customers. There was the guy who kept a suitcase of different-size dildos and paid Johann to insert them (into the client), from smallest to largest. "Boring," Johann said. "Who wants to look at someone's asshole for two hours?" Then there was the guy from Pasadena, a postal worker named Howard who lived with his parents. When Howard's parents were away, Johann received a call and a request to meet Howard in a particular Bob's Big Boy.

"Ronnie. This guy makes me eat everything on the menu while he watches. I eat pancakes and eggs and ham and toast and a turkey sandwich and French fries and a big piece of apple pie with ice cream. He drinks coffee. We go to his house and he takes off all his clothes. Now, Ronnie, you have to understand, this is the ugliest man God ever created. He is seven feet tall. His nose, Ronnie…no man ever had a bigger nose than this. You look at him and you think a big crow has landed on his face. His ears are tiny. They stick out sideways. Ronnie, no one can love this man. Maybe his mother. But he has the biggest dick you ever saw. Twelve, thirteen inches. No one in a porn movie has a bigger dick than this. So he takes off his clothes. I stay dressed, in my boots, my leather jacket. He watches me. He jerks off harder. He says, 'Johann. Did you weigh yourself this morning?' I say, 'Yes, Howard. Right after you called me.' He says, 'How much did you weigh?' I say, 'One hundred fifty-two pounds.' He starts jerking off harder. He shows me a scale, in the bathroom. I step on the scale. Now Howard is all covered with sweat. His hand is pumping his dick a hundred miles an hour. He says, 'Johann. How much do you weigh now?' I say, 'Now I weigh one hundred and fifty-*four* pounds.' He jerks harder. He can barely talk. He says, 'You gained *two pounds* at Bob's Big Boy!' And then he comes all over the place."

"How much do you charge him?"

"Four hundred dollars. I could charge more. I go the whole day without eating. But Howard works in a post office. I can't take all his money. You see, this is my problem. I'm compassionate."

Johann rolled toward me. He wrapped his hands around my penis, which had deflated. "I like talking to you. You're a nice guy. I wish I could stay here all night."

"Well. You could." Johann seemed to consider the offer. I added, "If you need to charge extra…"

His eyes narrowed, calculating—I imagined—hours and

25

dollars. I expected him to name a price for the service known as an "overnight."

"No, Ronnie," he said. "You need to sleep, and why should you spend so much money when I am tired?" He kissed me on the forehead. Perhaps it was the crack, but I recalled my childhood, a winter night in a small town with a clear sky, the warmth of my moonlit bedroom, overheated by a coal furnace, the consoling voice of my mother bidding me to say my prayers, and her lips on my forehead.

I counted money as Johann pulled on his black jeans. There's something about a stack of twenties on a bedsheet that sucks the romance out of a room. Johann folded the bills into his pocket without verifying the amount, giving the wad of cash no more significance than his keys and some change. I watched as he finished dressing, his gestures precise: running two fingers of each hand through his hair, pressing it behind his ears.

I stood to say goodbye, wanting to kiss him on the lips, but did not dare. Experience had taught me that the only taboo between prostitutes and johns is a kiss on the mouth.

"Are you going back to the office?"

"No way. I see one customer a night. I am not an ATM machine."

We hugged, and my lips brushed his neck. "Call me," he said. "I gave you my pager number." He smiled. "But don't use 911."

The next day I was thickheaded and impatient. A script meeting seemed to go on for hours. I was trapped in a plush office with seven well-groomed colleagues drinking Evian, debating a single line of dialogue: "You shouldn't have left us, Mama." A vice president of production, in a Laura Ashley dress and cowboy boots, had proposed another version: "Mama, it was wrong for you to leave us."

I said nothing. My head was pounding, and I was nauseous. Familiar feelings, after a night of martinis. But there was another feeling under the normal hangover feelings, a dryness in my throat and a jittery, recurring tingle in my extremities: the residue, I surmised, of crack working its way through my system. Across from me, a bespectacled, chubby senior executive peeled a banana. Her brow scrunched, she pondered the competing lines of dialogue. The problem confounded her, the way some people are confounded by the question of God's existence. As she placed the banana in her mouth, I thought of sex with Johann and the feeling of hurtling through space.

I covered my face with my hands so no one could see me laugh. They did see, however, that I had covered my face with my hands. Someone asked if anything was wrong. I kept my hands on my face, enjoying the warmth of my own recycled breath. The room fell silent. I realized I had reached a potential turning point. I might remain as I was, keeping my hands on my face, until someone had the presence of mind to call 911 and summon a team of paramedics. They will whisk me to an emergency room and then to a psych ward and possibly a rehab. It will be dramatic. And it will be over: the searching for drugs, the hangovers, the hours in hotel rooms crashing from speedy coke, the degrading moments with prostitutes who declare their heterosexuality the moment you try to kiss them, the promises to God never to do it again. I thought, *If I keep my hands on my face, I will be saved.* People forgive these minor breakdowns. In show business they admire them.

I remembered Johann, his freckled shoulders, and the smell of cologne in his crotch. He said he hoped to see me again. He wanted to show me his master's leather mask. I remembered how he'd held my flaccid penis while humming "Happy Birthday." I had his pager number in my wallet. They will make me throw it away, the people in the psych ward and the rehab. Certainly, that's the kind of thing they make you do, throw away the pager numbers of prostitutes with good drug connections. Johann promised the next time we got together he would come prepared, with powdered cocaine. "More sophisticated," he had said. "Like you, Ronnie." I imagined making love to Johann with my heart surging after two thick lines of coke. *I will kiss him deeply and for a long time. I will somehow come to possess him or convince him that he ought to possess me.*

I dropped my hands from my face and delivered a revised line of dialogue: "Mama, you shouldn't have left us. It was wrong!"

Relief flickered over the faces of my colleagues. I wasn't going mad. I was being *creative.* The chubby senior executive swallowed a chunk of banana and declared, "It's a compromise. But it works."

Four

I returned from Los Angeles to my home in upstate New York, abandoning Johann and fantasies regarding space travel or earthly rescue. I had work to do.

I struggled to make changes on the Appalachian romantic comedy script ("Mama, you shouldn't have left us!") but my work was hampered by the awareness that it was one of those hopeless studio projects that no one in charge intended to make. The subject of the script was the only truly taboo subject in Hollywood: poor people. Really poor people, the kind of people who buy toilet paper in bulk. I had been told Ashley Judd was interested in playing the lead, but I had trouble envisioning Judd wrapping her arms around a 24-pack of Quilted Northern.

A year after an Academy Award nomination, my career was sputtering. The success of *Philadelphia* had endowed me with a momentary—and, apparently, illusory—sense of power. I thought I might continue to combine entertainment with issues of social justice and churn out one winner after another, successful pictures that would "change things." I spoke arrogantly to producers, telling them I had a mission to create art that offered "hope." I wrote a script about a sexually promiscuous blind woman falling in love with a minister who had lost his faith (an homage to W. Somerset Maugham's *Rain*). I adapted a nonfiction book about schizophrenics, tilting it toward self-righteousness as I condemned current trends in mental health care. And I rewrote the script set in

29

Appalachia, trying to expose the dead-end nature of minimum-wage service jobs, although I made the female lead a
spunky feminist who just happened to be blessed with a beautiful singing voice. One by one I handed in drafts of my social-
ly-conscious-but-entertaining-enough-for-the-mainstream
screenplays. And one by one they elicited ho-hum responses
from studio executives. Each rejection provided an excuse for
a day or two of drinking and drugging that left me foggy-
headed. I found myself trying to write with shaking fingers
and blurred vision, turning out enough pages to stave off the
inquiries of anxious producers.

The decline in my professional fortunes was matched by
the emptiness of my personal life. I divorced a partner of
many years and lived alone in my upstate New York farmhouse. Questions from friends about the nature of the
breakup drew surly responses from me, and the more sensitive
among my friends stopped asking. The truth was, I had no
answers, only vague feelings of restlessness, disappointment,
and a desire to be alone or, at least, to spend time with people
who did not count my martinis. It occurred to me—as my
boyfriend's moving van pulled out of the driveway—that I
would no longer have to hide packets of cocaine at the bottom
of my underwear drawer.

My property south of Woodstock occupies sixteen acres
that encompass a blue stone quarry. In the 1940s the quarry
workers hit an underground spring, and the cold water rush-
ing to fill the blue stone basin ended the site's usefulness as a
source for New York City sidewalks. Eventually, a farmer
named Maddaloni built a three-story, cinder-block barn next
to my house and filled it with chickens. The chickens were
gone in 1988, when I bought the house from a potter, who
took up windsurfing and moved to Cape Cod.

Heron dive into the water in my quarry, coyote howl in
the woods behind my house, deer consume my hostas, and

once an owl crossed my driveway, with a body the size of a small dog and a wingspan as broad as my car. There is no evidence of human life visible from the windows of my house, except for one yellow porch light that beckons through stark trees in winter. Occasionally the quiet is interrupted by a distant chain saw, a confused rooster crowing in the afternoons, and, on Friday nights, someone's garage band murdering Aerosmith tunes.

That winter, I worked most mornings and left my house in the afternoons to purchase supplies. I lived on prepared food from upscale venues, dishes with chickpeas, couscous, and feta cheese. My refrigerator was filled with soggy paper containers, a rock-hard pint of frozen tofu dessert in the freezer, and a bottle of gin at eye level on a shelf of its own.

In the evenings, as the sun dimmed, chills crept through my nervous system, and I had trouble taking a deep breath. My house is full of windows and I avoided them. I had the creepy feeling of being watched by the darkness—not by someone *in* the darkness, but the darkness itself, as if it might enter my soul through my eyes. I recognized these feelings as symptoms of mental illness; I had, after all, done all that research for my script on schizophrenia. But this knowledge did not blunt my feelings of hopelessness.

I thought of calling Johann. Staring at his pager number written inside a matchbook, I wondered why this stranger held sway over me. Did this speak to his power or my desperation? I couldn't deny that my guts fluttered each time I thought of his commanding voice and his hand wrapped around my leg. But I imagined he would be impatient with my call. I was three thousand miles away—I couldn't be calling to solicit sex. Escorts are notoriously wary of purposeless conversations, and they warn against them in their classified ads with the phrase "Serious calls only." I savored my memory of Johann and didn't want it diluted by his impatient response to an out-of-the-blue call. You don't say to a hustler, when he wonders aloud why you've dialed his number, "I just wanted to hear your voice."

Most days I managed to wait until five o'clock to mix a pitcher of martinis. The glasses and the pitcher were kept in the refrigerator with olives and vermouth. The martinis gave me courage to look out the windows, and I watched the evening wrap around the pear and crab apple trees in my backyard. There might have been a murmur of traffic from Route 28, half a mile away, but often there was only silence.

I developed the habit of stalking about my house with a drink in hand, wearing thermal underwear, examining remnants of a former life—mine. There was a beeswax candle presented by an Easter-weekend house guest, a tie-dyed yarmulke from a seder that coincided with the harmonic convergence, an enameled candle snuffer presented at a dinner party. Often I contemplated driving to a nearby restaurant for solo dinner at the bar, but by seven o'clock and the third martini, I no longer was hungry, which was fortunate, as I no longer was fit to drive. By nine o'clock, if there was no cocaine in the house, I lay unconscious on the sofa.

✳ ✳ ✳

I was born with a "lazy eye"; a weak muscle causes my right eye to drift outward, especially when I'm tired. I heard my mother say, when I was grown, that she ought to have made me wear a patch as a child, over the good eye, to force the weak one to correct itself, but for some reason never got around to it. This is exactly how she put it, as if repairing a bad eye was a pesky chore, like throwing out a box of old dishes that clutter the basement. I suppose this attitude explains why I never received braces for my overlapping front teeth.

My wandering eye gave people the impression I was staring past them, lost in my own world. Considering I had so little interest in the things that fascinated everyone else when I was growing up—football, fishing, hunting—this impression was more accurate than not. I was terrible with balls. I couldn't throw them or catch them; they always seemed two feet ahead of—or behind—my hands. In a more compassionate time, in a place other than the company town of a major coal-mining concern, someone might have figured out that my lazy eye contributed to my ball-catching trouble. But in those days, in that town, my "refusal" to catch a ball was deemed a matter of willfulness and brought forth expressions of disgust from the other ball-handling boys and their rugged, tobacco-chewing, coal-mining fathers.

My dissymmetric eye was not a peculiar pathology among my kin. My grandmother had her right eye sewn shut by a doctor from a clinic for coal-mining families after he botched her cataract operation. My Uncle Lee had been blinded in one eye by a firecracker. His useless, scarred eye remained in its socket, murky and turned downward.

On both sides of my family there was typical, small-town trouble: illegitimate cousins, occasional senility, aunts in nursing homes wearing diapers. None of it was regarded as too serious or unusual, and I managed—at a young age—to carve out a niche among my relatives as eccentric. I was, after all, the only boy to participate in the annual Greene Country Bituminous Coal Queen Pageant. I impersonated Sonny Bono, pretending to play the piano, while my best friend (the official contestant) lip-synched a Cher ballad, wearing a glossy five-dollar wig. We—I mean, she—did not win.

As a teenager I wallowed in emotion. At a church camp on a hillside near Somerset, Pennsylvania, I accepted Jesus into my heart as my personal lord and savior, collapsing into the arms of a counselor, grieving for Christ's suffering and mortification and wailing with gratitude and surrender. It was quite a show. Other campers (including my friend, Frances McDormand, whose father, Vernon, fulfilled the role of camp director) accepted Jesus into their hearts—during our makeshift communion service, using crumbled saltines and grape Kool-Aid—with a distracted glance at the stars, as if contemplating pillow fights and softball games, while I howled away.

For my hometown church, I wrote and staged a futuristic drama depicting a world where Christianity was banned. At the play's climax, I turned off the lights, plunging my parents and their contemporaries into darkness. I had planted strobe lights above the altar, and I started them flashing while playing the most raucous selections from *Jesus Christ Superstar* at the loudest possible volume. At the play's end, when my star lay on the floor of the sanctuary, after her character had been beheaded for refusing to deny Christ (I was influenced by the PBS miniseries *The Six Wives of Henry VIII*, which prompted a lifelong fascination with Anne Boleyn), I faced the congregation, wearing an I ♥ JESUS T-shirt, begging them to come forward to save their souls. No one stirred. But later, at the coffee social, my parents were congratulated for having a son who "ought to go into drama or something like that."

I entered the University of Pittsburgh to study theater but was frightened by the worldliness of the students (I spotted one of them reading the magazine *After Dark*, ogling the photograph of a near-naked bodybuilder). I fled the bohemian theater department for the flannel-shirt safety of a creative writing major. The writing students were ill-groomed and politically progressive; they honored my coal-mining heritage. They encouraged me to write about it and I did, creating stories about the women back home who suffered wordlessly, felt unloved, and struggled to keep their houses clean of coal dust. I sublimated my emotional needs behind the needs of my characters and toned down the drama. I realized most people suffered not from life-and-death decisions made while staring down the executioner and his ax, but from *in*decision, from hopes never pursued and lives that somehow got out of hand.

I came out of the closet. It was the late 1970s and I hung

out with people who read Adrienne Rich and Virginia Woolf. I was working-class and I was homosexual and I was an artist. In other words, I was multiply oppressed and therefore, among my crowd, popular and admired. I discovered a gay bar in my neighborhood called the Tender Trap and just about moved into the place. You had to knock on the door and announce yourself to a formidable African-American lesbian bouncer who peered at you through a peephole. I began to drink and discovered the "click" that bourbon and tequila delivers, that Tennessee Williams writes about in *Cat on a Hot Tin Roof*, the moment in which self-consciousness and interior editing fades away. After a few hours of drinking at the Tender Trap, I ventured home with men I'd just met. When they held me, I remembered the arms of my church camp counselor, and my weeping and surrender to Christ in those arms. It was glorious to be held, to submit to penetration, to perform acts of love on my knees.

In the 1980s, I lived in New York City and drank huge frozen margaritas at Caribbean-themed restaurants and snorted cocaine like everyone else. My friends and I talked for hours on cocaine and danced. My career took off and I spread my money around—as Dolly Levi suggests, like manure—with elaborate dinners in Manhattan restaurants and rented houses in the Hamptons. I began to carry my own brand of tequila to parties. People gave me cocktail shakers for birthday presents and, once, a silver flask. I met my boyfriend and our families accepted us and we shared Christmas dinners and Passover seders. We moved into the farmhouse near Woodstock and grew our own basil, hosted swimming parties in our pond, and talked of adopting children. I switched from margaritas to martinis and argued with bartenders about stirring and shaking.

Alcoholism snuck up on me. It seemed that everyone was drinking but I was the one who crawled under the dining table to sleep at the feet of my embarrassed friends. I was the one who—as the drunken chef at a summer barbecue—let the swordfish steaks fall through the slats of the gas grill. With a Corona in one hand and tongs in the other, I plucked charred hunks of fish from the lava rocks and arranged them onto a platter. I was insulted when my guests turned them down.

There seemed to be one day in the early 1990s when all my friends gave up drinking and cocaine, and focused on gardening, raising children, and pursuing master's degrees. I decided to find new friends. While traveling to New York City and Los Angeles for business, I became a regular customer of notorious establishments populated by prostitutes and drug dealers. I detoxified on airplanes, with flight attendants pressing cold compresses to my forehead. I missed family get-togethers or passed through them sullen and hungover. I wrote melodramatic letters of apology to my boyfriend, filled with promises that were broken within a few days. Frequently I came down with the flu. Eventually my boyfriend left, and I put away his baking dishes and cookbooks and took to keeping a fifth of Bombay Sapphire gin in the refrigerator, with a bottle of olives, seeking out drug dealers who made home deliveries.

This is the life I returned to, after meeting Johann in Numbers: slogging by day on screenplays that might never be filmed and haunting my house at night, stoking self-pity with gin and cocaine, dreading my impending deadlines and restricting conversation to plaintive monologues delivered to three anxious dogs.

And then, one zero-degree evening in February, at about five o'clock, as blue-silver light haloed the trees of my backyard and my house filled with dreaded, mocking shadows, I wrapped a belt around my neck and tried to hang myself from the second-floor balustrade.

Five

My friend and carpenter, Armand, a Cajun artist with improbable green eyes, arrived to collect some tools. I climbed down from the makeshift gallows when I heard his truck in the driveway. I must have looked a mess—with a scratch at my throat from the belt's buckle and lips that were chapped and crusty—for Armand averted his eyes. But it wasn't the first time he had caught me at the end of a binge.

In the seconds that passed before either of us spoke, I told myself there was no reason to raise an alarm. The attempted hanging was not a genuinely suicidal act; my feet dangled briefly and remained close to the nearest stair. And I had been calm during the act, watching and doing at the same time. But fear overwhelmed feelings of embarrassment and I blurted, "I just wrapped this belt around my neck."

Armand, who was taking Prozac, remained calm. He suggested I look up a shrink in the Yellow Pages. He loaded his table saw into his truck, giving me another bit of advice. "See a psychiatrist if you want drugs. Therapists and social workers can't write scrips."

To my knowledge, no member of my family had ever consulted a therapist, though I have a vague memory, circa 1963, of my Aunt Margaret being "sent away" for a few weeks. She was married to my Uncle Lee (with the downcast dead eye), my mother's baby brother, who turned violent when he got drunk and drove his car over neighbors' lawns. My mother disapproved of her brother, sometimes seemed to detest him,

37

although she gave me his name (I'm Ronald Lee), and one can imagine therapeutic sessions devoted to this fact. One Sunday on our way to church, we passed a house with its front porch propped with fresh lumber, and my mother identified it as the scene of my uncle's latest spree. My mother, stoic when she wasn't suffering one of her "nerve attacks," marched defiantly into church to stare down the busybodies. But after the service, in the privacy of the family car, she reverted to disdain and for her wayward brother: "He drove your Aunt Margaret to the nuthouse. She wasn't crazy. She was humiliated. She went to Western Psych just to get away from that drunk."

Before my aunt turned fifty, she died of breast cancer. I'm sure my mother believes Aunt Margaret got cancer to avoid another humiliation perpetrated by my uncle. In my family, you can die, literally, of embarrassment.

According to his classified ad in the Yellow Pages, Dr. Yu was a psychiatrist, acupuncturist, and herbalist. More to the point, his office was a mere two miles from my house. I shared the waiting room with a hulking teenager who leaned forward, scratching his ankles. He wore no socks in February. I wore my grandfather's hunting jacket and Versace corduroys.

Dr. Yu emerged from an office and waved the boy inside. Once the door was closed, I heard him speak angrily to the boy in exclamations such as "Don't be stupid!" and "Stop scratching your ankles!" The boy emerged in ten minutes, bolting for the front door and slamming it hard, rattling Chinese prints on the walls. The doctor waved me into his office.

Dr. Yu wore aviator eyeglasses, and a shank of black hair dangled over his forehead. He began our session in a straightforward manner: "Tell me what is wrong with you." Before I could answer, the telephone rang. I was surprised when Dr. Yu picked it up. He spoke Chinese to someone for several minutes. I assumed it was an emergency, justifying the interruption of our session. However, he ended the conversation in English: "Don't forget a pint of half and half." He hung up the telephone and studied me.

"Oh, right. Well... I wrapped a belt around my neck."

Dr. Yu scribbled on a notepad with a drug company logo. "Anything else? How was your childhood?"

"Perfect," I answered.

Dr. Yu wrote it down. "What about your love life?"

I wondered if sessions with prostitutes constitute a love life. "I date now and then. I'm single. I don't think the belt thing has anything to do with that." Silently, I mined my recent past for a singular event that might explain my current state. A few unproduced screenplays seemed insufficient. There was the divorce, but I'd been the one who had provoked it. I considered mentioning my drinking and drug abuse, but abandoned that idea when I realized the doctor might suggest I stop drinking and taking drugs. But I had to give him *something* to work with.

"A couple of years ago I wrote a play. It got bad reviews."

Dr. Yu slapped his hand against his forehead, an eureka gesture. "Ah! You are an artist. I know many artists. If you have a dinner party, you should always invite a few artists. They are unusual. Very sensitive, however. One bad review and out comes the rope."

A door behind Dr. Yu opened, and a Caucasian couple walked through the office wearing benevolent smiles, like parental angels blessing Dr. Yu's new patient. They passed through a second door, to the waiting room. The corpulent boy with no socks had returned, slumped in a chair, clawing at bare skin showing above his shoes. They said hello to the boy, who scratched harder.

"Never mind them," Dr. Yu instructed, referring to the Caucasian couple. "He had a hip replacement and can't use the front steps." Just before the door closed, he yelped at the teenager, "Stop scratching!" The boy burst into tears.

Dr. Yu sighed. "You have no idea what I go through around here."

At Dr. Yu's request, I summarized my career and the events surrounding the failure of my play. He nodded occasionally and used a gesture of his hand—shaking his fingers as if they were wet—to urge me to keep the story moving. "I want to get the whole picture." I told him about the play, how it had been inspired by a trip to Rome with my now-absent boyfriend, and the sight of an African nun prostrating herself before a procession of bishops in St. Peter's on the Day of the Epiphanies.

"I wanted to write about transcendence."

"And what do you wish to transcend?"

"You mean, personally?"

He fixed me with a dumb stare, the counterpoint to his shaking-finger gesture. Now, I surmised, he expected me to elaborate.

"When I'm in my house I feel like I'm in a tomb. I can hear myself breathe. But when I'm out in the world, with other people, everything they say grates on my nerves. People are so *annoying*. So I go back to my house. I go to bed and I listen to myself breathe." I got The Stare, demanding elaboration. "It doesn't feel like I'm living the life I'm supposed to be living. I don't know. Maybe I ought to entertain more."

Dr. Yu's eyes drifted to a window, to a view of the street, blackened by Highway Department ash, and sooty cars passing by, heading for the Hudson Valley Mall. His jacket was threadbare and his grooming incomplete; an annoying patch of stubble had escaped the morning's razor. He implemented the impatient hand gesture. "More you. Your work."

I drew a blank. Shouldn't we be talking about something more significant than my career, some subject beneath the surface, the discussion of which will provide relief? I had come for help; my motives were sincere. It's frightening to wrap a belt around your neck and hang from a stair rail in your own house, daylight fading on the snow outside and your dogs pawing at the door, desperate to escape. Yet here I was, reciting my résumé. I remembered Johann asking, "Do you know any stars?"

Do you tell a psychiatrist to change the subject? Or is that as much a gaffe as demanding a kiss on the lips from a prostitute? I kept finding myself in situations in which I had no idea how to proceed. Life had become dreamlike, the kind of dream in which one stands on a tennis court, facing an opponent, unfamiliar with the rules of the game or even the proper way to hold the racket.

The phone rang and I nearly jumped out of my chair. "Very loud," Dr. Yu said, reaching for the phone. "Very irritating." Again, he spoke Chinese. I liked the sound of it. I liked not knowing what he was saying; it was restful. I closed my eyes and thought of Johann and tawny port wine.

✳ ✳ ✳

My second night in Los Angeles with Johann began in Numbers, where he introduced me to his friend Peter, a Czech bodybuilder who begged me to put him into the movies. Peter wore a neon-yellow tank shirt. His arms and every visible inch of skin were hairless and alabaster, a statue with a beautiful smile. We sat in a red leather banquette and ordered dinner. Peter ate only protein: steak tartare, filet mignon, cheesecake, and a glass of milk.

Johann told me Peter was a master as well; he was straight and avoided contact with clients. Peter corrected him: "I'll piss on them if they want."

Johann eyed the hustlers loitering about. Tonight he was jaunty, more confident than usual. He wasn't looking for work like the others; he had me. He gave me the rundown on the boys, who was a crackhead, a porn star, who was kept, had a heroin habit, was married. According to Johann, none of them had any ambition other than finding a sugar daddy. Johann made it clear he wasn't looking for a sugar daddy; he'd made it this far under his own steam.

"All the way to Los Angeles, Ronnie. Europe, New York, Dallas, L.A. I move in one direction: west. Next stop, Beverly Hills."

"Do you know what I think?" Peter pointed his steak knife in my direction. "I think you need *two* men tonight. Two masters."

Cutting his pork chop, Johann offered no reaction. Was he testing my loyalty? Perhaps he didn't he care about the details of the evening as long as his portion of the proceeds wasn't affected.

"No man can serve two masters," I said, watching Johann carefully, hoping for some sign of approval.

Peter continued selling himself. "Look at this chest. You want to see my abs? You want to see my butt? Hard like this table and smooth like baby's skin. Look what Johann eats. Sauce and butter and potatoes. Look what Peter eats: meat, baby. All meat, and raw, with blood. I never drink alcohol, I never take drugs. I'm pure, baby. Pure master. Plus my dick is bigger than Johann's. My dick is bigger than any dick in this room. *I'll* be your master, baby." He threw a napkin to the floor. "Pick it up, you piece of shit."

I appealed to Johann. "Don't we have an arrangement this evening?"

Johann offered a compassionate smile. "But, Ronnie, in Numbers you have to make a choice. Just like life."

Peter was gorgeous; his black nipples showed through the tank shirt and his chest was so developed I imagined burying my face in the center of it, licking his smooth skin, sliding my tongue down ridges of his abs, or kneeling at his feet, lost in subjugation.

I caught Johann staring at the candle flame, his features bearing a caul of sadness. The expression was fleeting; the moment he realized I was looking his way he reapplied his trademark, cocksure smile. The smile was the thing I paid for and was available to anyone in the room for a price. But the source of Johann's sadness intrigued me, the mystery of it held me in thrall; I sensed this commodity wasn't available to the general public, not a retail item, and *it* was the prize I sought.

I stared Peter down. "Say something in Latin."

Peter drew a blank, then grappled for a comeback. "I can tell you to eat me in Czech."

"Latin."

Peter floundered. "I can say suck my cock in Czech, German, Italian, and Portuguese."

The game was over. "Sorry, Peter. I'm with Johann this evening. I guess you'll have to pick up that napkin yourself."

Johann slapped the table with both hands, shaking with laughter, as Peter bent under the table for the napkin. "And while you're under there, *Master,*" Johann said, "suck my cock in English."

After dinner, Johann suggested I drink tawny port wine. "It suits you."

At this point I had only one answer for any of Johann's suggestions: "Yes, Master."

"And pay the check so we can get out of here."

"Yes, Master."

"We cannot stay up late. You have a plane to catch."

"Yes, Master."

"And, Ronnie. Tonight, no drugs."

I hesitated, imagining the guest room in my agent's house, the Pottery Barn sheets and coral-colored closet, imagining Johann's freckled skin and my cold hands. Johann justified his position. "Why should you give all that money to a drug dealer? You throw it away on bad people like that. Look at Peter, a good man..." At the bar, Peter prospected a fat albino customer who looked like a Swedish Luciano Pavarotti. "Give Peter the money for his rent. Give me the money for school."

I sipped port wine. It was thick, buttery, and smooth but lacked the brain-rattling punch of tequila or gin. Johann wanted me sober; he was protecting me. Johann was greedy; he wanted my money. In life, as in Numbers, one has to make a choice.

I startled Johann by placing my hand over his, on the table, in full view. "Why do you think my hands are always so cold?"

Johann lowered my hand to his crotch. "Because you do not keep them in the right place."

I made love to Johann that night without drugs. It was awkward. Neither of us had an orgasm. Johann let me off the hook. "You are nervous about flying tomorrow." He left as he had left the night before, grooming in the mirror, patting the folded wad of twenties in his front, right pocket.

✳ ✳ ✳

Dr. Yu's hand hovered above a prescription pad as he finished his telephone conversation in Chinese. He hung up and delivered his verdict.

"You suffer from Impostor Syndrome. You believe you are not intelligent, not talented, not worthy of the success you have achieved. You fear that your true self will be discovered at any moment. This is normal but not pleasant. I am giving you a prescription for Clonopin. It reduces anxiety. So does acupuncture, but I doubt you will be receptive in your current state. I am also giving you a prescription for Paxil, an antidepressant. It might make you impotent. If it does, let me know and we'll try something else. Begin taking the Clonopin and the Paxil this afternoon. Come to see me next week. And please write a check for one hundred and fifty dollars."

I noted that Dr. Yu's hourly rate matched Johann's but kept the observation to myself.

Dr. Yu paused, writing the prescription. "Do you abuse alcohol or drugs?"

"Oh, God, no. I'm essentially very conservative."

He handed me drug samples along with the prescriptions. Immediately my mood improved. I decided there must be something to the therapeutic process after all. I felt better, lighter, and I had been required to give so little, a few innocuous entries from my biography, the kind of things one tells strangers on airplanes.

I remembered something Johann had said about his clientele. "The best ones, Ronnie, are the ones who just want to blow me. I sit back and think about good times and beautiful men, and sometimes beautiful women and their breasts. It's funny, don't you think? They pay me so much money to relax."

Six

Midnight Gathering of
WOMYN
to Welcome Spring!
African and Brazilian Drummers
Chanting, Singing, Praying—
Overlook Mountain

—FLYER STAPLED TO TELEPHONE POST IN WOODSTOCK, NEW YORK

That March the nights were chilly and damp. People commented on the vernal equinox, as people from Woodstock tend to do.

I abused the anti-anxiety medication Dr. Yu had prescribed, swallowing three or four at once, washing them down with tawny port wine. I tried the antidepressant, Paxil, but it made my stomach queasy. I endured another appointment with Dr. Yu, but cringed when he suggested "exploring" my childhood. I declared there was nothing to discuss, that I had grown up in a small town where the streets were safe and no one locked doors at night.

"Trust me," I said.

He gave me a version of The Stare—the look that was meant to elicit elaboration—but added a skeptical narrowing of his eyes, turning The Stare into A Challenge. I glanced to the prescription pad resting on the stained desk blotter, mentally calculating how many Clonopin remained in the little orange bottle I kept in the glove compartment of my car. (You never know when a traffic situation is going to make you nervous.) Even for drugs, I was reluctant to dredge my past for decades-old injuries. My problems were present-tense: I was lonely, I felt my career slipping away, I suspected I wasn't *really* a good writer, and I'd squandered whatever talent I had in Hollywood trying to please people who were impossible to please.

"I hate people who complain about their childhoods, don't you?"

"Funny question to ask therapist," Dr. Yu replied. "Why you come here? Let me remind you. You want to hurt yourself. You put belt around your neck. Where do you think that comes from?"

"The belt came from Barneys."

Dr. Yu added a new expression to his repertoire. He pursed his lips and looked to the ceiling. He was Puzzled. Or Impatient. Or Impatiently Puzzled.

"How you like the Clonopin?" he asked.

They're fantastic, especially when I take four at a time with tawny port wine. "They're okay," I answered. "I mean, I think they're helping a little."

"Hmm," he said. "I think you like Clonopin." Perhaps Dr. Yu wasn't so puzzled after all. "I'll renew the prescription— one more time. But let me give you a piece of advice. What you are hiding from me, you are *not* hiding from yourself."

The woman who had been my mother-in-law for seventeen years went into the hospital, and everyone prepared for her to die. She was in awful health, barely able to breathe from emphysema; she coughed, wheezed, choked on phlegm, regularly spit mucus into a balled-up tissue. She was confined to a wheelchair and required round-the-clock oxygen. She lived nearby; my ex-boyfriend and I had moved her to Kingston from a tenement in the Bronx. Though he and I split up, Gloria depended upon my continued attention when I was able to give it. When she entered the hospital, going into the intensive care unit, I roused myself to visit.

I entered the room where Gloria lay. She had been intubated and couldn't speak. She possessed a memorable voice, the kind Raymond Chandler imitators call "whiskey-soaked," although Gloria didn't drink; it was one vice she never cultivated. Her eyes widened at the sight of me, and I took her puffy hand in mine.

Alan, my ex, stood at the foot of the bed, massaging his mother's feet, which, swollen and purple, had passed the point of looking human, as if she were wearing boots. She thrust a finger in my direction.

"What does she want?"

"I think she wants me to ask you something."

Gloria slapped the bed, impatient. Alan responded with sarcasm (his standard weapon of defense): "Sorry, Ma, I haven't mastered finger-pointing language." She held a bloated forefinger against a bloated thumb and scribbled in the air, then pointed at me. I ventured an interpretation: "Maybe she wants a pen and pad so she can write."

Gloria nodded while rolling her eyes, managing to convey at once relief for being understood and contempt for its taking so long.

Alan asked, "How did you figure that out?"

"She pointed at me, and I'm a writer. And…" I held a forefinger against my thumb, scribbling in the air. "Isn't this the universal symbol for writing?"

Alan said, "I thought she was asking for the check."

I heard from Johann on a damp afternoon. The phone rang while I was searching the house for an umbrella. I was on my way to the hospital, taking a turn in Gloria's deathwatch. Immediately I recognized the male growl with the faint European accent. "Ronnie, you forget about me already?"

I played a game. "Who is this?"

"This is your *master*."

"Johann?"

"How many masters do you have?"

"Where are you?"

"Where else?" he sighed. "The City of Angels, and I don't mean heaven."

I jumped to the conclusion that he was calling for money. It wouldn't be the first time a hustler had called hoping for a "loan." I was a notorious overtipper, a quality appreciated by prostitutes. One had called from jail asking me to pay his bond. Another, a porn star known as the White Mandingo, reached me from a crack house in Long Island and asked to borrow five thousand dollars. He said he planned to open a fitness studio. "I'm letting you in on the ground floor."

Even under ridiculous circumstances, I couldn't say no, outright. So I lied. I told the jailbird my father had died and I was on my way to his funeral. I put off the White Mandingo's request with the news that I had been diagnosed with prostate cancer. He responded, "This might be the time to make a wise investment."

To Johann, I spoke stiffly, now suspicious: "What do you want?"

"Ronnie. I want you to pray for me. I'm depressed."

Johann described his troubles. When his mother died two years ago, he couldn't afford to fly home for her funeral. He was haunted by this omission. "So I get depressed on Mother's Day."

"It's March."

"European Mother's Day. It comes earlier than yours." He feared that his brother, younger by four years, had been selling their mother's furniture and precious keepsakes to finance a career as a race car driver.

"What's his name?"

He seemed caught off-guard by the question. "His name? What difference does it make? Ronnie, you know why I think of my mother today?" His voice was low, confessional.

"Why?"

"My teeth hurt."

"You think of your mother when your teeth hurt?"

Johann's Schwarzenegger accent nearly disappeared. I was talking to a little boy. "Maybe it sounds funny, but my mother was a dentist. She was *my* dentist. And I can't let someone else touch my teeth. I don't want to cheat on her. This is ridiculous, right? Ronnie, are you laughing at me?"

"No, Johann." I wasn't.

"I have not seen one dentist since I come to America. My teeth are rotten. Nothing hurts like a toothache, you know? And when I go to the office… Well, Ronnie, you can imagine, with my work. Wearing that mask and fisting someone. With a toothache. I have to listen to them whimper, you know. But they don't want to hear *me* complain. The master never complains. The master never feels pain."

"I'll send you money to go to the dentist."

There was a long silence.

"Johann?"

"You think I call you for *money?*"

I felt small. "No, of course you didn't."

"Ronnie," he said. "This is something you must remember about me. I am a prostitute. But I am not a gigolo. I will tell you the difference. A prostitute makes you pay for sex. But a gigolo makes you pay for friendship. Ronnie, I promise you, my friendship is free."

He hung up.

✳ ✳ ✳

Like Johann, Gloria had an appetite for pleasure. She lived to eat in restaurants, gnawing the bones of lamb chops and, when she was done with them, tossing them aside, once over her shoulder, like a Roman emperor. She was built like an Eskimo, squat and low to the ground; she dyed her hair a brassy copper shade, frequently went about without wearing her false teeth, and painted her lips scarlet. She gambled. Her boyfriend, Sonny, was a numbers runner. She adored her son, although she contradicted every statement he uttered, even the acknowledgment of a beautiful day ("Beautiful, schmootiful"). And I believe she loved me, although she never quite trusted me. She suspected that I—a successful goyim—would leave her son and herself someday, when the right fellow Gentile came along.

When she wasn't in the hospital, Gloria lived in a senior citizen apartment building that stood next to a funeral parlor. She lived in self-imposed semi-isolation, alienating her neighbors with insults and blurted declarations of contempt. Once, a fellow resident greeted Gloria in the elevator with the question, "Where are you going?" Gloria replied, "Hell. You like that answer?" She lectured the old ladies in her building, cursed them, laughed at them, and denounced them in her version of a stage whisper that could be heard across the dining hall.

Gloria used her mouth more than anyone I'd known: eating, coughing, smoking, choking, barking orders. To see her in her hospital bed, orally encumbered, was heartbreaking, with the respirator's tube down her throat, another tube taped to her mouth to suction saliva. It was like seeing Itzhak Perlman without hands.

She tried communicating with a tiny notepad and pen. There were single word demands for supplies: "Ice. Blanket." There were orders to change the channel on the eternally playing television: "*Jeopardy! Oprah.*" There were questions that seemed innocent on the surface but resonated with Gloria's generally impatient and resentful personality: a niece's name, for example, with several questions marks scrawled after it, as if to say, *Where the hell is she?*

Once, when a disconcertingly cheerful doctor disappointed Gloria, declaring that she was not ready to be extubated and would *not* be extubated until her blood-oxygen count reached a level that "makes me happy," Gloria jotted something on the notepad and jabbed it toward me, waving a hand dismissively toward the smiling doctor. Silently, I read the words she had written: "Fucking moron."

Alan was a steadfast companion to his mother, and I relieved him or kept the two of them company. Daughters and cousins came and went, but often it was the three of us—Alan, myself, and Gloria—marking time, riding the roller coaster of hopeful signs and signs that pointed in another direction, the optimism and deflation of terminal illness.

I met Alan in film school; he was my first New York City boyfriend. For our third date, he took me, a boy from Pittsburgh, to the Bronx to meet his widowed mother.

It was Super Bowl Sunday and Gloria made pot roast. She nearly choked when I asked for a glass of milk. I didn't understand why she kept muttering, "Milk and pot roast, oy," throughout the meal, oblivious to Alan's shushing. She must have said it twenty times, "Milk and pot roast, oy," like a mantra, while lighting a cigarette or glopping gravy over mashed potatoes, glaring at me.

I redeemed myself during dessert (Italian pastry from the corner bakery), when I glanced at the television and noted, "Pittsburgh just got a first down."

Gloria growled an order: "Say that again."

"Pittsburgh just got a first down. They're on Miami's twenty-yard line."

She threw her hands into the air, flinging cigarette ash across the room. "He knows football!" She was incredulous. But the exclamation was followed by an accusation. "*You* don't play football. Not a skinny thing like you." She sized me up with narrowed eyes; clearly I was trying to pull a fast one.

"I played saxophone in the marching band. I must have seen a thousand football games."

She nodded, putting it together. "Pennsylvania. Small town. Milk and pot roast." She paused for more calculations and added: "I bet your parents eat lima beans."

"As a matter of fact, they do."

She clapped her hands, turned to Alan and announced, "Lima bean eaters!" Never was I a mystery to Gloria again. I was a foreigner, an element that didn't belong; I was too WASPy, too successful, too quiet, too blond, too Protestant, too moody. I exercised too hard, ate too little, did too many chores. I fussed too much about the garden, my antiques, and my clothes. But eventually I was promoted to second favorite, after her son. And I was always offered the first slice of pot roast at family meals.

Food, music, and movies defined Gloria's life. When she described her elopement, to Louisiana at the age of fifteen, she recalled poorboys and crawfish. When she thought of her dead husband, "Mushy," she thought of Alice Faye singing "You'll Never Know." She spoke of Barbara Stanwyck and Gary Cooper as if they lived in the apartment next door. "She loved Robert Taylor," she said, speaking of Stanwyck, who happened to be my favorite. "But it wasn't about sex between those two. Everything is about sex these days. Back then people had class; they were sophisticated." She made this claim sitting at her coffee-stained kitchen table in a blowsy house-dress, tapping a cigarette into an overflowing ashtray, while the television blared a football game and a cockroach meandered up the wall.

Gloria rolled her eyes when, early in our courtship, Alan informed her I hoped to be a screenwriter. "Like William Holden in *Sunset Boulevard*?"

Alan answered, "Who does that make me?"

But no one enjoyed my success more than Gloria. Alan and I took her to Lincoln Center to see Jonathan Demme's film *Melvin and Howard* at the New York Film Festival. Demme had optioned a screenplay of mine. Alan worked as an intern for the festival and pressed the script into Demme's hands, provoking a severe look from his boss. But Demme liked my script, and I got a development deal, an agent, and three tickets to the premiere of *Melvin and Howard*.

Gloria's response to the film was tepid. "I don't get it," she declared. "Howard Hughes is dead." She was confused by the dreamlike ending of the film, in which the deceased Hughes and Melvin Dummar take a final ride in Dummar's jalopy.

"It's a ghost," I retorted, in an exasperated whisper, hinting to Gloria to keep her voice down. But Gloria did not respond to hints. In fact, she did not respond to commands.

"A *ghost*?!" she exclaimed, causing people in long dresses and tuxedos to turn our way. "That's some kind of *farkuckt* ghost!"

At the cocktail reception I slipped away from Alan and his mother, collecting congratulations for my good fortune from Demme's colleagues and film festival staffers. When I heard a commotion, coming from the center of the room, I wandered toward it curiously, realizing too late that Gloria was the cause. I found a circle of people gathered around Mary Steenburgen, who played Melvin Dummar's wife and was several months pregnant.

Steenburgen was cowering as Gloria tried to flatten both hands against her belly. Alan tugged at Gloria's wrists, trying to pry her away, but Gloria clung to Mary Steenburgen like a python to a rabbit. I feared the actress might faint or go into labor. "It's going to be a boy!" Gloria shouted. "Look how high you're carrying it!" I tiptoed into the crowd and spent the rest of the evening pretending not to know Alan or his mother.

Years later, when Gloria lived in Kingston, she kept a photo in her apartment, taken at a White House dinner, with Alan and me flanking President Clinton. Gloria played a game with visitors, using this photo. When a stranger visited—a neighbor, a social worker, a health care aide—Gloria talked about her children and finally asked her guest (a.k.a. the sucker),

"Would you like to see a picture of my son?" When the stranger responded affirmatively, Gloria pointed toward the photo of Alan and myself standing on either side of the president of the United States.

"Which one is your son?" the gullible visitor might ask.

"Well," Gloria retorted, thrilled to be showing off and making someone feel stupid at the same time, "he's not the one in the middle!"

Gloria and my mother—one of the "lima bean eaters"—settled into an uneasy friendship. My mother strove for propriety above all but allowed, for the sake of peace, Gloria's public rebukes or explosions of enthusiasm to pass without comment. (My father found everything Gloria said to be hilarious, and he shared her passion for poker and lottery numbers, which irked my mother.) Now and then my mother was roused to self-defense. "I like lima beans and I'm not ashamed of it," she claimed over Thanksgiving dinner. "What's wrong with lima beans?"

One Christmas Eve, Gloria and my mother found a basis for mutual regard when they agreed (over some glasses of wine) that men were, for the most part, useful but disappointing. As Alan and I cleared the table, Gloria and my mother (Thelma—"A lima-bean-eater name if I ever heard one," according to Gloria) recalled teenage flirtations in the World War II era with boys in uniform, carried out in soda shops and diners; these flirtations had ended when each of them met the man she married. Gloria and my mother fell silent. I sensed these women nearing seventy were questioning the choices they had made forty years ago.

We heard my father and Gloria's boyfriend, Sonny, in conversation in the living room, recounting recent visits to the doctor, the ailment and diagnosis, and the prescription medicine or outpatient surgery that had succeeded or failed.

My mother groaned, "Oh, Jesus. I'm so tired of hearing

that man talk about being *sick*." Then, she made a startling confession: "One of the clerks at the Payless shoe store flirts with me every time I go in there. I think he wants to have an affair with me."

I was shocked. "Mom!"

My mother seemed to remember where she was and backtracked: "Oh, I didn't mean it. I would never…"

Gloria leapt to her feet, raising her arms over her head and shaking her fists at heaven. "Do it, Thelma!" she cried. "Before it's too late. *Live!* You got to *live!*"

Often I visited Gloria in the ICU after dinner in a local restaurant. For her entertainment, I recalled my meal, item by item: poached salmon in parchment paper, blackened string beans, mango sorbet. (I left out the martinis.) I described the menu and tried to remember the evening's specials. I outlined my decision-making process, why I chose one dish over another: meat loaf for comfort on a frigid evening, or steamed rice and vegetables when I felt I'd been eating too much meat loaf. It seemed a strange way to pass the time, even torturous, considering Gloria couldn't eat, except for a few chips of ice. But she pinched my arm if my attention drifted or she suspected I'd neglected a course. As if she was eating the meal herself, she couldn't get enough.

When Gloria closed her eyes, drifting into morphine-inspired dreams, I popped a couple of Clonopins and lolled in a chair beside her, entertaining dreams of my own. I conjured sunshine, taut skin, salt air, the smell of fried food. Every dream wound its way toward a pair of black, laced boots. I thought of Johann's muscular back, the smell of his cologne. I wondered how his skin might taste after a day at the beach, sandy and warm. I tried to resist these Johann dreams, tried escaping into other realms, planning solo excursions to a rain forest or a set of ruins in Central America. Sometimes I thought, begrudgingly, about work. But I was drawn back to

Johann, to his freckles, his biceps, the blond hair on his upper thighs, his commanding voice growling a command. *Submit, submit, submit.*

I abandoned the purgatory of Gloria's room, finding a public telephone. I dialed Johann's pager and punched in my home phone number, adding "911" to the numerical message. Then I realized it was a pointless act; if Johann answered my page, I wasn't home to take the call. I tried to think of a way to cancel the page but couldn't, and I headed back to the ICU, where Alan was having a hushed conference with an excited Indian doctor. Alan held his fist to his chin, staring at the doctor's shoulder while she spoke in run-on sentences. I saw Alan squeeze his nose and realized he was trying to pinch back tears. I entered Gloria's room and found her awake, roused from her dreams as I had been from mine. She tapped the tip of her white tongue against her chapped upper lip, demanding a spoonful of ice.

When Alan entered the room, he gave me a sideways glance that implied bad news. He searched through a box of cassette tapes and began playing swing music from the 1940s. We stood on either side of Gloria's bed, holding each of her hands. When Gloria closed her eyes, Alan mouthed the doctor's prognosis: "Tomorrow."

"I'll be right back," I said.

I found a men's room and locked the door. Gloria's death was tangible. It boiled down to a single word, a date on a calendar. Alan planned to leave upstate New York when Gloria died. The era of our family unit was over, like the era of swing bands and Alice Faye. It struck me as selfish to view Gloria's impending death in terms of my own needs. But how else to view it? What is the death of someone you love and share a history with, if not an intensely personal affront?

I removed my glasses and—with the same split focus I had experienced while wrapping a belt around my neck, participant and observer—I whacked my head against the men's room wall, rattling the paper towel dispenser. I did this three times.

I sat on the closed toilet to catch my breath and regain balance. "This is weird," I said aloud. "I'm going to have to do something about this." I imagined telling Dr. Yu about this new habit I'd acquired. I tried to anticipate the look he would utilize in response. Would he be Puzzled? Impatient? Or would he offer something new, a look that corresponded with my own feelings about this act. What's the universal look for You Disgust Me?

I ran water over my face, straightened my hair, and returned to Gloria's room. For the rest of the evening I was quiet. I watched everything from a distance, which seemed, considering the circumstances, a safe place to be.

Seven

It is my impression of Key West that one can drop dead on Duval Street, the main commercial avenue, crowded with souvenir shops and groggy tourists, and no one will notice. Everyone is too drunk, too happy, and too weary from the sun.

I promenaded next to Johann, feeling his sun-warmed, muscled arm brush against mine, watching tourists clear out of his way. Johann's headlight eyes were hidden behind wraparound, Euro-style sunglasses, but this did not dilute his superior, semidetached, potentially threatening aura. He paid particular attention to anyone passing on *my* side, who might intrude into my share of the sidewalk. He appeared ready to pounce. One oversize Midwestern mother pulled her baby's stroller into the street, making a path for us. I imagined Johann as something from the science fiction movies he loved, my humanoid protector, with killing, laser eyes.

My reconciliation with Johann took place the day after Gloria died. Alan and I had watched her go, life signs ebbing to zero. Alan stroked her hand as she slipped away. "Everything's all right, Mom. Ron's here with me. We're together, just like you wanted."

"Ronnie, you paged me?"

The phone rang while I unknotted my shoes, still grimy from the New Jersey cemetery, where we'd buried Gloria.

"I just came from a funeral."

"Who died?" he asked, alarmed.

"My mother-in-law. My ex-boyfriend's mother."

"As long as it wasn't *your* mother."

This distinction struck me as arbitrary and cold-blooded. "I loved her as much as I love my own mother."

"No, Ronnie," he argued. "You don't love anyone like that. You live in your mother's belly. When you are born, you rip her apart. Did you see the movie *Alien* when the monster comes out, how those people scream, and all the blood? This is what your mother goes through, and then she feeds you with her breast. Nobody else feeds you with her breast. Ronnie, is your mother dead?"

"No."

"Do you tell her you love her?"

"I suppose I do. Sometimes."

"Your master says you must call your mother and tell her you love her *every day!*"

I heard whimpering in the background. Johann turned away from the phone. "Shut the fuck up." Then, to me, lowering his voice: "I'm calling from a client's house. This guy is getting on my nerves. All he wants to do is jerk off."

I heard some arguing, the opening and closing of drawers. Johann reported: "He ran out of lube. You won't believe it. Now he's using hair conditioner. Ah, Ronnie. When do you come to L.A.? Give me a break from these losers."

"I thought you were mad at me," I said, remembering our last phone conversation, his clarifying the difference between a prostitute and a gigolo and hanging up.

"I turn the other cheek, like Jesus."

With my hospital-room dreams of salty air and sunshine on my mind, I ventured, "Can you meet me in Key West?"

"Ah, Ronnie! You want to have fun in the sun? All right!"

The growl in his voice, when he said "fun in the sun," stirred a craving.

"Can you bring something?"

He toyed with me. "Sure, Ronnie. I bring my gorgeous body and my super personality."

I was silent.

"What's the matter, Ronnie? You want more than my body and my personality? Okay, I bring my beautiful blue eyes. How many days do you want me? I can't be away from the office too long. I have to pay my tuition."

"I'll take care of you."

In the background Johann's client begin to whine. "Wait a minute, Ronnie. I have to do something with this guy." Johann put down the phone. I heard scuffling, a door open and close. He returned to the phone, out of breath.

"Okay, Ronnie. Now we can talk. I put the asshole in the closet."

The tourists of Key West, suntanned to the shade of a saddlebag, streamed along Duval Street, ogling shop after shop hawking the same five T-shirts. Johann and I invented a game, predicting the respective fates of passersby.

"Melanoma," I diagnosed, for a suntanned matron in Prada with skin resembling the shell of a coconut.

"Heart attack. Boom!" Johann snapped his fingers, eyeing an overweight Marlboro smoker.

An Italian fashion victim, cell phone pressed against his temple, inspired us to proclaim simultaneously: "Brain tumor!" We leaned against a parking meter, laughing, attracting attention.

"Ronnie. I need to eat."

Johann's voice was hoarse; he'd been up for two days before meeting me in Key West. A party in Pasadena, he explained, and he'd nearly missed his plane. When I chastised him, he snapped, "I only went to the party for *you*, to get you the drugs you care so much about."

Under palm trees at an outdoor café, I watched Johann eat three soft tacos, rice, refried beans, a green salad, chips with guacamole, and a bowl of vanilla ice cream, along with two Diet Pepsis. Across the street, drag queens and muscled boys flowed in and out of a daytime bar for tea dance. The disco beat and occasional cackle of laughter underscored my lunch with Johann.

"Ronnie? You want to go to the party?"

I *always* wanted to go the party, and I always wanted to leave moments after I arrived. What do the Buddhists say? There is no unhappiness without desire.

But today was different. I watched the bronzed barhoppers, with flat bellies exposed beneath cropped T-shirts, but wasn't drawn to them. I had everything I needed within reach.

"No, I don't want to go to the party." Johann hailed the waitress and demanded chocolate sauce for his ice cream. She claimed there was no chocolate sauce on the premises. Johann lifted the menu and pointed to a description of the peanut butter pie which was served with chocolate sauce. A minute later, the waitress delivered a ramekin filled with steaming fudge.

"You see, Ronnie. Johann asks for something, it appears. You sure come on vacation with the right guy."

We shared a tiny room at a guesthouse in Old Town. It happened to be the same room I'd occupied a few years before, when Tropical Storm Andrew turned into a hurricane and I had been evacuated from the island.

"Evacuated means they throw you out," I explained to Johann. His belongings were scant: two pair of Guess jeans, white T-shirts, black socks, and a leather face mask with a zippered mouth.

The master's mask made me nervous. "I don't think I'm into it."

Johann shrugged. "I want you to have all the options." He hung the mask over a lamp.

Later, I stood on the deck of our guest room, looking to

the garden and date palms clustered around the Jacuzzi. Guests had abandoned the pool for predinner showers. Inside the room, Johann lay on the bed, fully clothed, arms behind his head. "Okay. I had lunch," he said. "I suppose *you* want dessert."

The proposal of sex, in near daylight, in a mostly sober state, caused me to fidget and my mouth turn dry.

"Perhaps, Ronnie, you need a little encouragement."

Johann dug into the bottom of his boot, retrieving three aluminum foil packages. "I was stupid to use foil. I didn't worry about it until I am halfway through the metal detector. Then I think, *Shit! I am fucked!*"

Something bothered me. What did he mean, "use" foil? The dealer packages the drugs, not the client. Was Johann dealing?

He continued with his airport story. "But nothing happens. No alarm. Everyone smiles. This big fat lady says, 'Have a nice trip.' I am always protected, Ronnie. God loves Johann. Say it."

"Didn't the dealer wrap the packages for you?"

Johann's smile was frozen, but the ice-cold look in his eyes betrayed the smile. "Ronnie. I gave you an order. Say 'God loves Johann.'"

I realized I might push him toward a genuine reaction, something so impulsive it could not be mistaken for playacting. "You must have me confused with some of your sicker clients."

Johann dangled the foil packages. "Say it or I flush them down the toilet."

"Go fuck yourself."

A blotch of red colored his cheeks. I wondered if he might strike. He seemed to be making a decision—how to play the moment. Finally, he erupted.

"Ronnie, I like you! You're crazy!"

This declaration of affection took each of us by surprise. Johann deflected his bloodshot eyes.

"I'm different from your other clients, aren't I?"

"Yes, Ronnie," he answered. "Except for *one* thing."

"What's that?"

"You all ask the same question."

Moving toward the stash, at four-thirty in the morning, searching for a rolled-up twenty-dollar bill, I vowed, "One more, but this is the last."

Johann chimed in. "Let's make a promise. If we do one more line, we *ruin* our vacation."

Three hours later, Johann turned the final package inside out, scraped free the last nuggets of powder, and rubbed them beneath his tongue. "Well, Ronnie," he said. "I think we ruin the vacation."

With the sun peering around the edges of the windows and sleep out of the question, Johann told me the story of his life.

He was adopted by an engineer and his wife, who later became a dentist. Two years later the couple was surprised with a pregnancy, and Johann's brother was born. Johann sensed his father's preference for the younger son, his own blood. Johann's mother never showed a hint of favoritism, and for that Johann loved her deeply.

"What were their names?"

We were whispering. Guests moved about in adjoining rooms, running showers or clomping down the stairs to a breakfast buffet.

"I called them Mother and Father."

"What did other people call them?"

"I thought *I* was telling the story."

Johann's father and brother rebuilt wrecked cars and raced them on weekends. Johann assisted his mother when she went to dental school, cooking while she studied at the kitchen table. Johann never wanted to be seen stirring soup by his father, so his mother took his place at the stove just before dinner. She served, and Johann's father and brother never knew whose hands had prepared the meal. "This secret she took to the grave."

But Johann was no sissy. He excelled at soccer. He skied and had girlfriends.

"Are you bisexual?" I risked his wrath, interrupting, but my hand was stroking his thigh. I wondered if he preferred a woman's hand.

"I like women from the waist up. I like men from the waist down."

"I don't get it."

"What don't you understand, Ronnie?" Johann adopted his bored tone, as if we'd covered this ground a million times. Perhaps he had, with other curious clients.

"You're not gay..." He remained silent, conceding this fact. "But you put me in your mouth." What was I hoping to hear? *Only you, Ronnie. I do it only for you.*

"Ronnie. A dick is strong. It stands up. But a woman..." He searched for words. "It's an opening. You go in."

I spoke softly. "You can go into a man." In truth, no one was going inside anyone this morning, with our penises defeated by cocaine. But I wanted to float the offer for future reference, like a deal memo. *I'll give this to you.*

"I don't get fucked." He misunderstood. Before I could correct him, he added, "I save that for when I have a real boyfriend."

Johann wanted to live in America. He was tired of competing for his father's attention. He saved his money and flew to New York, landing a job as a bellhop at the Peninsula Hotel. "You don't have to speak English to carry a suitcase." He learned the new language quickly and became a popular employee. He found another exiled European, named Gabor like his brother, who was fun ("a maniac") and they took an apartment together. Johann sent money home. He and his brother exchanged letters, and he felt he was earning, finally, his father's respect.

One night, Gabor took Johann to a bar on 53rd Street

called Rounds, filled with two kinds of patrons: young, handsome men with suntans and muscles, and older men with money. Gabor explained the commercial nature of the establishment, and Johann's life changed.

"Think about it, Ronnie. At the hotel, some guy gives me two dollars to carry his suitcase. I go to the bar, I find a nice guy who gives me two *hundred* dollars so he can blow me. This is when I realize, America is the greatest country on earth."

"Rounds. It's a hustler bar. I've been there."

Johann smirked. "Big surprise."

Buyers and sellers entered Rounds through a heavy wooden door, walking past a long bar, toward a lounge and a dining room. There were candles on the tables, and sometimes a piano player abused a baby grand. The silver wallpaper and black lacquered furniture represented someone's version of art deco, a look that my dead mother-in-law, Gloria, called "piss elegant." The older men wore polo shirts and sports jackets. The younger ones wore polo shirts and denim jackets. The hustlers at Rounds referred to themselves as "escorts." They were blunt in the way New Yorkers are blunt.

Once, I encountered a shiny-haired, broad-chested young man leaving the lounge. He planted himself in my path and declared: "My name is Dennis. I'm Italian-Greek, with a smooth body, five foot eleven, a hundred and seventy-two pounds, uncut and really thick."

"Pleased to meet you," I replied.

Dennis pressed closer. I smelled garlic on his breath. "Are you interested in me?"

"I just walked in."

"Window-shopping is for Bloomingdale's," he said, swaggering toward the bar.

Johann quit his bellhop job to work at Rounds. "Next time I go to the Peninsula Hotel, someone will carry *my* bags." Johann wasn't a bodybuilder, like many of the escorts; his torso and arms were taut from playing sports, not bulging from steroids and pumping iron. He attracted business by adopting an aggressive style and playing up his European origins. In the hottest months he wore black boots with thick soles and a leather jacket. Self-conscious about his small hands, he allowed the sleeves of his jacket to dangle past his wrists. Later he learned that small hands were a bonus, attracting certain customers who desired those hands inserted into them.

"I don't like fisting," he confided. "How can these guys take it, Ronnie?" He tapped the inside of his elbow. "All the way up to here? I try to get out of it, if I can."

"How do you get out of it?"

"I try to get them interested in a dildo, if they have one."

"What if they don't have one?"

"I go to the kitchen and look for a vegetable. The green one…"

"A bell pepper?"

Johann rolled his eyes. I made a second guess. "A cucumber?"

"I make it a game," he continued, putting on the Master's voice. "You pissed me off, you piece of shit. I'll shove something up your ass that will make you scream. Come here, bitch, I'm gonna give you this…"

"Banana!"

Johann slapped his face with both hands. "No, Ronnie, not a banana! Too soft. You get it in, but maybe you don't get it out. Then you have to call 911."

I imitated the master's voice: "Hello, 911? I want to report a banana stuck in someone's asshole."

"You think it's funny. But these are the problems of my job."

Johann lay still and naked. I wanted to rest my hand on his chest, but, thinking of the hundreds of hands that touched him when he didn't want to be touched, I held back.

Within seconds his breathing came regularly as if he'd fallen asleep. But he wasn't asleep; his body remained taut, he cleared his throat too consciously. Perhaps this was his way of ending his working day, turning off the meter.

"How can you sleep?"

The master's voice: "Clean conscience."

I remembered the title of a Japanese movie I'd seen in college and said it out loud: "*The Bad Sleep Well.*"

"You think I'm bad?" Now his voice was injured, childlike. *The many moods of Johann.*

"It's the title of a movie. Have you seen any Japanese movies?"

"Sure. *Godzilla.*"

Johann rolled away and I noticed that his hair was thinning at the crown. I wondered if he was older than he claimed, 26.

Emboldened by exhaustion, I slid my hand between Johann's thighs, just beneath his butt. Surprising me, Johann adjusted his legs, lifting them, allowing me to slide my hands farther, until my fingers grazed his balls. He clamped his legs shut, flexing the muscles of his inner thighs, showing off his strength. I pondered the significance of Johann's invitation, the opening of his legs to me, the warmth welcoming my hand. Soon Johann's breathing took on the throaty exhalation of genuine sleep and I watched his chest rise and fall.

They say you know a dog trusts you if it will sleep in your presence with both eyes closed. What does it mean if a man like Johann drifts to sleep while you're holding his balls?

Eight

...the citizens are well acquainted with mischief,
but at a cost.

—John Hersey, *Key West Tales*

"Why do the ugly guys always have big dicks?" Johann asked, in the garden of our guesthouse, crouched at the edge of the tiled "lagoon." He referred to fellow guests, a couple from Virginia, naked in chaise lounges, with sagging chests, potbellies, and huge rubbery penises that they slathered with suntan oil, taking advantage of our "clothing-optional" pool deck and grounds.

Halfway through the day, Johann and I had mustered the energy to leave the room. We devoured submarine sandwiches made by lesbians at a deli across the street. (For the rest of our vacation, we referred to sandwiches as "lesbians," asking each other, "Do you want to eat a lesbian?")

Johann swam laps across a pool that was never meant to be treated so seriously. I floated on an air mattress, noting the reactions of the naked and nearly naked guests to Johann's athletic body and the bulge in his black Speedo. Johann kicked his feet as he swam, splashing guests who repositioned their chairs. I apologized. They answered "No problem" and continued ogling Johann.

After his swim, Johann and I clung to the same air mattress, dangling in chlorinated water. The sun and the lesbian sandwich had ameliorated most symptoms of my hangover—the muscle

aches and scratchy throat—though I was exhausted and might
have returned to bed with some encouragement. But the evening
stretched ahead, hours to spend with Johann. I had to stop
yawning.

Johann raised the ante. "What plans do we make, Ronnie?
What do we do for fun in Key West?"

I was daunted by the responsibility of entertaining Johann.
He *was* the entertainment, watching him move, listening to his
stories. I knew nothing of his tastes for pleasure outside a narrow range of activity: finding drugs, using drugs, having sex
on drugs.

Johann spurted pool water, missing my face.

"Ernest Hemingway lived in Key West. We can take a tour
of his house. It's full of cats. They're inbred. Most of them have
six toes on each foot."

He lowered his mouth to the pool's surface, churning
water.

"We can watch the sunset from the docks. Everyone goes
and takes pictures. It's like a street fair."

More bubbles, the sound growing louder, like a lawnmower
hitting a patch of tall grass.

"Maybe I can find someone who has connections and we
can party some more. I know these two guys. I met them a
couple of years ago…" Johann was growling now, as he blew
bubbles. I seemed to be striking out and feared I'd offended
him, returning to my obsession with drugs, as if I was
unable to enjoy his company without getting high. I backtracked. "Forget that," I declared. "I'm giving up drugs and
alcohol."

Johann shot pool water through his teeth, catching me in
the ear. "You'll give up drugs, Ronnie, the day I grow a pair of
tits."

He grabbed my shoulders and tried to dunk me; we
laughed and wrestled like twelve-year-olds. One of the naked,
oil-drenched Virginians glanced from Johann to me, regard-

ing me with envy. This pleased me. It feels good to have something others want, even if you don't really have it.

While Johann washed the chlorine from his hair, I lay on the bed and pondered whether we might live together. On the plus side, our bathroom habits were dissimilar, therefore compatible. I showered and groomed quickly, while he required the bathroom for long sessions of scrubbing, combing, powdering, and gelling. I never spoke of my bodily functions and always locked the bathroom door, but he approached the toilet with a flourish, a gladiator entering the arena, grabbing a stack of magazines and declaring, "I'll see you in a few days."

There was the question of the location of our home, geographical as well as cultural. What universe might we occupy together? I nursed a fantasy in which I moved to Los Angeles and became Johann's manager, sitting at the bar in Numbers, negotiating with clients and paging Johann after an hour, his signal to end the session and return to me. I stumbled into a melodramatic version of this fantasy, in which I followed Johann to the bar each night, begging him to give up "the life," and watched forlornly as he ducked into limousines with cashmered customers. Bets were taken among the other hustlers as to which rich client would steal him away. This version of my imagined future with Johann ended in homicide and suicide, his and mine respectively.

Johann stood naked before the bathroom mirror, steering a cheap, plastic comb through his hair. One rebellious strand pointed to the ceiling. He exhibited a saint's forbearance running the comb along his skull to clinch the stray. I tried to imagine him living with me in Woodstock, standing naked in front of *my* bathroom mirror, but this image was replaced with one of him tilling my garden in his storm-trooper boots, with Japanese beetles, drawn to his designer cologne, drowning in his gelled hair like prehistoric bugs fossilized in amber. And how would I introduce him to my Woodstock friends?

"This is Johann. He's really a nice guy, once you get past the leather mask."

I angled my head to look past the flesh-and-blood Johann to his reflection in the bathroom mirror. Why was I obsessed with this man? I asked myself this question—silently—several times. On the third or fourth repetition, my mental voice acquired a Chinese accent, the exasperated voice of my acupuncturist, herbalist, and psychiatrist, Dr. Yu.

On my third visit to Dr. Yu, I was greeted in the dreary waiting room by the overgrown boy who scratched his ankles. In the warmer days of spring his limbs were bare, beneath fringed cutoffs, and he scraped the skin of each entire plump leg. He startled me by speaking.

"Dr. Yu is my father," he said. "And I'm okay with patricide."

I wasn't sure I'd heard him correctly. "It's okay if I go inside?"

"Patricide!" he shouted. "Don't you speak English?"

I had a steaming hangover, and my sinuses were clogged. I had no patience for anyone's insanity but my own. "Stop scratching!" I shouted at the boy. He looked injured and bolted from the room, slamming the door so hard the whole building shook. From one of the mysterious rooms at the back, where acupuncture was administered, I heard someone moan, and I wondered if the boy slamming the door had caused Dr. Yu's hand to jerk while inserting a needle. It was funny to think of that chain reaction: from me to the boy, to the slamming door, to Dr. Yu's hand, to a needle sliding into exposed skin. My anger had wafted freestyle through the house and found an innocent target. This event struck me as some pathetic metaphor for the Truth, that life was a series of needle pricks, illogical, undeserved, and unpredictable.

Inside Dr. Yu's office I explained my theory, concluding, "It makes no sense for us to sit here and try to figure out the *cause* of all these pricks of the needle. They're random. You just have to take them and move on."

Dr. Yu entertained my soliloquy while resting his chin on his hand, covering one eye with extended fingers. "One problem with theory. If you hold needle in your own hand, and you keep sticking yourself with it, this is not random. This is *you* sticking *you*. And this is no good. And this we can fix."

"How?"

"Find needle and throw it away. Find all the needles. I'll give you example of needle. You think you can buy love from prostitute..." (I had mentioned, in a previous session, that I sometimes pursued paid-for sex. Dr. Yu had focused on this minor foible, as if he had discovered King Solomon's mine.) "...because you control the prostitute, so everything safe. But prostitute never love customer."

"That's not—"

Dr. Yu marched through my attempted interruption. "*Prostitute never love customer.* This is truth older than Confucius. So you try new prostitute. Not work again. Hurt again. Try again. But this is not the needle. Needle is the *reason.* Why you don't try to love man who is not a prostitute? What are you afraid of? Something you do not talk about with all your stories. Something from long ago that gave you pain. And you associate this pain with love. This is the needle, my friend. Your secret fear. Let me ask you a question. When you hire these prostitutes, do you ever ask them to slap you around maybe, or tie you up?"

"Absolutely not! Never. It's just sex. It's nothing!" I realized I was shouting, perhaps undermining my denials. To change the topic I let loose a bored, exaggerated sigh. "I think we've had enough of this needle metaphor, don't you?"

I dragged Johann to tourist attractions. The sun was brutal, and he turned grumpy, dabbing at sweat rolling down his neck. He didn't speak except to read signs in a devastating monotone: "The Southernmost Liquor Store," "The Southernmost 7-Eleven." He was not impressed by Key West's latitudinal significance. He came alive only as we faced the ocean at a rocky beach and read the words painted on a concrete wall: "Ninety Miles to Cuba."

"That's what I will do, Ronnie. I will swim to Cuba."

"It's *ninety* miles."

He flexed his biceps. "I think I will like Cuba."

"Are you a socialist?"

He gave one of his contemptuous chuckles. "Ronnie, all prostitutes are capitalists." A hefty, gray-haired couple wearing T-shirts bearing the maple-leaf flag of Canada eavesdropped as Johann continued, "Anyone who sells himself…"

Johann's voice faded, and an unfamiliar expression clouded his features. He looked uncomfortable, even insecure. He glanced at the Canadian couple: pale, plump, benign, grandparental. They held hands. Johann seemed to regret declaring himself a prostitute in front of them. He bit his lower lip, as if he wanted to take back the words.

But this moment of self-doubt, if that's what it was, passed. He smiled and spoke in the master's voice: "I want to be in Havana the day Castro dies. That will be some party!" The Canadian couple nodded in agreement.

With the evening stretching ahead and Johann stationed in the bathroom with a year's worth of *Vanity Fair*, I called a local couple, Kenny and Emmanuel, to arrange an evening on the town. Emmanuel, once a Latin beauty, had come to America via the Mariel boatlift; he was a lush and a flirt. Kenny, from Southern money, was genteel and long-suffering. We'd met two years earlier at a bar during an evening of drag karaoke. Kenny and Emmanuel were well-known hosts in gay Key West, famous for parties centered around some hilarious activity, such as a nude scavenger hunt. They were happy to hear from me and, as fate would have it, were throwing a party that evening.

"We're invited to a party."

Johann emerged from the bathroom. "An orgy?"

"A going-away party."

Johann looked puzzled, as if he could not comprehend a party that was not an orgy.

"They're crazy guys. You'll love them. It's a theme party."

"And what is the *theme* of this party?"

"White trash." Johann flopped onto the bed, covering his genitals with a washcloth. He arranged the washcloth so that it formed a diamond, with the topmost corner pointing to his belly button. "The guest of honor is moving to a part of Key West that's called New Town. The people in New Town are low-class and trashy. They have carports and satellite dishes and riding lawn mowers. That's why it's a white trash party, because she's turning into white trash."

Johann folded the washcloth onto itself into a tiny parallelogram.

"Whatever makes you happy, Ronnie."

Kenny greeted us at the door wearing a stained undershirt and boxer shorts, a TV remote tied to one wrist and a empty beer can tied to the other. He was curly-haired, flabby, and allowed his belly to hang over his belt. "Don't want no faggots in my house!" he declared, attempting to sound like a redneck. Kenny spoke with sibilant s's, which doomed his macho pose.

Walking to the party, I'd wondered how to introduce Johann at our first public appearance; that is, outside of a hustler bar and a couple of restaurants. I might say anything. Kenny and Emmanuel were relative strangers, our acquaintance formed during a drunken night of karaoke. They knew little about me, beyond the fact that I could sing all the words to "Gypsies, Tramps, and Thieves."

But how to introduce Johann? I didn't dare call him my "lover," as he might panic and correct me on the spot. "Friend" was vague, boring. "Buddy" was ridiculous, something to call someone who fishes with you or hunts or bowls, not someone you have serviced until the carpet has left crimson divots on your knees.

"This is Johann. My..." Kenny eyed Johann with a blunt look of lust.

Johann finished my sentence, speaking in full Arnold mode: "I'm Ronnie's bodyguard."

The party was crowded and loud, and everyone was having a grand time. Music played on a loop, the theme song from the television show *The Jeffersons,* and everyone sang along: *Movin' on up, to the East Side... To a dee-luxe apartment in the sky-y!*

The guest of honor was a woman named Gina, who wore curlers in her hair and a fluorescent pink Care Bears sweat suit that was several sizes too small. She kept a cigarette dangling from her mouth, and when she needed a fresh one, she bent over, allowing her sweat pants to slide down her bottom, exposing the cleft in her ass, which she referred to as her "cigarette holder." And there, in fact, rested a cigarette, which she plucked and shoved into her mouth while the party guests screamed and applauded.

Johann spoke to no one. When Kenny offered a tray of hot dogs wrapped in pastry dough—"You faggots want a pig in the blanket?"—Johann scooped a dozen of them into his arms. He sank into the sofa and devoured the hors d'oeuvres. "We have real food," Kenny said. "That stuff's supposed to be ironic."

Emmanuel floated into the room in a McDonald's uniform. He was sinewy, and brown, with a dancer's posture. But tonight he wore a ratty wig in a hairnet, greeting guests with "Fries with your Quarter Pounder?"

Kenny explained, "Emmanuel had a terrible time deciding what to wear. I suggested the McDonald's thing. He *had* the uniform. But Emmanuel's from Cuba. He didn't connect

Mickey D's to white trash. Someone employed at McDonald's is, after all, employed. That's upward mobility in Cuba. That's the high life."

Emmanuel planted himself in front of Johann, cocked his head, and asked, "Fries with your blow job?" He wasn't deterred by Johann's blank stare. Having the attention of half the room, Emmanuel pointed to Johann's crotch and announced, "I bet it's *already* supersized!"

Seconds passed with everyone waiting for Johann to respond, and I began to feel dread. I recognized the look on Johann's face. It was the expression one sees on great, intelligent beasts at zoos when human spectators speak gibberish to them, calling them cute and asking their names. You can see the conflicting emotions in the caged beasts' eyes: bloodlust mitigated by pity. Johann licked pastry crumbs from his fingers.

"Get me a Diet Pepsi," he commanded, without irony.

Emmanuel's bravado wilted, as if he were a drunken party guest wearing a lamp shade who has caught a glimpse of himself in a mirror. When one is past forty, happens to be wearing a ratty wig and a brown-and-yellow McDonald's uniform, is slightly drunk and making half-witted jokes, it's fun only as long as everyone agrees that it's fun. Johann's contempt burst the proverbial balloon. The theme song from *The Jeffersons* started up, and someone moaned, "Oh, shut that damn thing off."

Johann pointed at me. "Ronnie? What do you need?"

I waved my plastic mug of margarita. "I'm all set."

Johann dismissed Emmanuel. "Just the Diet Pepsi."

Emmanuel staggered toward the refrigerator. People went back to their conversations, which now were muted. I heard the popping-open of beers. A group of drag queens, dressed as a ladies' bowling team, made for the door. Kenny tried to intercept them, brandishing Twinkies. "Aren't you going to stay for dessert?" There was a touch of panic in his voice, an awareness that a party simply can't survive a mass exodus of drag queens.

But the ladies declined the Twinkies and passed into the night, clutching vinyl bowling bags that doubled as purses. Johann rested his feet on the coffee table and flipped through a vintage copy of *TV Guide* with the stars of *Married With Children* on the cover, unaware the magazine was a prop.

I couldn't leave the party. I didn't want to be alone with Johann. I feared his assessment of our adventure, even a silent one, the look of exasperation, the sound of his boots on the sidewalk heading home. I drank the way alcoholics drink when a party dies, hard and continuously. I kept my distance from Johann, who fell asleep in a seated position on the sofa, head tilted back, mouth open, balancing a Diet Pepsi on his knee.

Kenny stuck with me while Emmanuel fluttered around the house, chortling at his own jokes, oblivious to the shift in the overall tone of the party. Kenny observed of his lover, "Emmanuel likes to have fun, no matter what." "No matter what" encompasses so much, I thought. Political upheaval, natural disaster, emergency surgery. I imagined Emmanuel being wheeled on a gurney to an operating room, cracking jokes. *No matter what.*

"No matter what," I said aloud. "I like that philosophy."

Kenny agreed. We were drunk. "Apply it to life."

"To love," I added, daring to glance at Johann. The can of Diet Pepsi on his knee leaned toward the carpet at a forty-five-degree angle.

"Yes. Especially to love." Kenny's mid-Atlantic, Southern accent was soothing and made him sound wise. For some reason, from another room, Emmanuel was crowing like a rooster. "When I left my wife…" Kenny read the confusion on my face. "Not Emmanuel. I mean, my real wife. A girl I met in Bible college. The mother of my children. When I left her for Emmanuel, it was like the world was going to end. I was a minister. We had a mission to a group of refugees from Cuba. They were locked up like criminals. They hadn't done anything wrong, at least not in the United States. Their crime was being unwanted in their own country. We took them food and clothes and copies of the New Testament. When I saw Emmanuel in that prison, when our hands touched as I handed him a New Testament, it was like something from the movies, like the sky opened for a revelation. I knew then and there I loved him. I know that sounds crazy, but it's true. I guess I was always gay, always felt uncomfortable playing husband and daddy. Don't get me wrong. I love my kids. I loved my wife. She's a fine lady. Superfine. But I was living in the wrong skin. Never could relax, take it easy. Because I was lying to myself and everyone else. But when I touched Emmanuel's hand—his hands were so soft for a man's. I think I love his skin more than anything else. Latins don't get wrinkles, you know, not the way we do. He'll get fat, but he won't wrinkle. My wife and my children suffered. They were innocent and didn't deserve to feel all that pain. But I had to be with Emmanuel, no matter what. I had to love him, no matter what. Now we're all friends. The kids love Uncle Manny. He's like their crazy Cuban Auntie Mame. My wife and I try to be friends. She still suffers. She still loves me. She can't help it. Just like I can't help it that I love Emmanuel. And you can't help it that you love your bodyguard."

"How do you know?"

"Do you think my wife didn't know I'd fallen in love with Manny? She started crying one day, standing at the stove, dropping hot dogs into the skillet. I hadn't done anything with Emmanuel. We'd only touched that one time. But she knew and I knew." He nodded in Johann's direction. "*He* knows."

"We have an unusual relationship."

Kenny smiled. "Probably not so unusual."

"You don't understand the situation."

Kenny replied, "Your secrets aren't as secret as you think." I remembered similar advice from Dr. Yu, about hiding something from others but not myself. Kenny gestured toward a movie poster on a nearby wall, *Rebecca,* starring Laurence Olivier and Joan Fontaine. "My favorite movie," he said.

"Great movie," I concurred, welcoming the change of subject.

"In the beginning, Joan Fontaine works for an old lady, right? Before she meets Laurence Olivier."

"Right."

Kenny quizzed me. "Do you remember her job?" I hesitated, and Kenny answered his own question. "She was a paid companion."

Nine

I started the morning with a tequila hangover, regretting the day before and my failure to entertain Johann. I had been too eager to please, dragging him to tourist attractions and ill-fated parties. I was wounded by his dismissal of my efforts, muttered before falling asleep: "Boring day. Maybe tomorrow will be better."

I decided to try a new approach: indifference. After all, I was paying him. Why should I work so hard to please? Wasn't that *his* job?

Ignoring Johann wasn't easy. He lay on an air mattress in the pool, blowing a pink bubble-gum bubble as large as his face, while I lolled in a chaise lounge, reading a biography of Martin Luther. Johann sustained the bubble for several seconds then plucked it from his mouth, admiring the way it caught the sun.

"Tell me this, Ronnie. Who blows bigger bubbles than Johann?"

I affected a bored tone. "No one blows bigger bubbles than Johann."

"I'm not bragging. It's a fact."

He showed no sign of registering my aloof posture; I resolved meet his detachment with my own. I searched for a way to seal this bargain with myself and found one, looking past the top of my Luther book. My feet and ankles, exposed to the sun, were shifting colors from pink to scarlet. It was time to cover them or move my chair. I lay still. The sun would do what it was meant to do—hurt me. I would allow my feet to burn in silence. *That will show him!* And later, I might bang my head against a palm tree.

I was trained at an early age to inure myself to pain. My brother, older by nine and a half years, lifted weights in the basement and listened to cool music, the Four Tops, the Temptations, Little Anthony and the Imperials. He drove a vintage blue-and-white convertible Corvette, studied advanced chemistry in front of the television, and was full of teenage, muscular rage. And for some reason, he hated the sight of me.

The nine-and-a-half-year gap in our ages indicated I was a "surprise baby." This was confirmed in a hospital waiting room, many years later, by my Aunt Eleanor, who joined me and my mother for a vigil during one of my father's angioplasties.

"Your mother cried the entire time she was pregnant with you," she explained.

My mother provided the punch line to this reminiscence. "Two weeks after we brought you home from the hospital, your brother marched into our bedroom, pointed to you in your crib, and said, 'Take it back!'"

My relatives guffawed. Staring at their contorted faces, I wondered, silently: Wasn't my brother—at age nine and a half—too old to make this naive remark? And if he really said it, hadn't it *worried* anyone?

Both my parents worked. This afforded my brother opportunity to enforce *his* house rules, which were malleable, baffling, and illogical. It was dangerous to speak when my brother didn't want to hear me speak. However, I committed a serious infraction if I failed to respond promptly to a question or replied in a "snotty" tone. Touching the television's channel selector, after he had settled on a particular program, constituted a capital crime.

Often I was guilty of breaking mysterious rules, things I

was meant to know but somehow hadn't learned. I was chastised for the way I walked (like a girl), my voice (like a girl's), the way I carried my schoolbooks (the way girls carry books). It wasn't unusual for my brother to flatten me to the floor, pin my arms with his knees, and press a sofa pillow over my face.

We played a game with a hard rubber ball (my participation was not voluntary). I might be alone in the backyard, my mother and father at work, when my brother appeared with one arm—his pitching arm—tucked behind his back. He began to count. "One…two…" I was meant to dart away, to avoid what was coming. I stumbled out of the sandbox and ran. When my brother reached three, he threw the ball. He was an athlete and could throw. Whether I was a foot away or several feet away, the ball left his hand at the count of three and I got it on the back, sometimes in a kidney.

For all the punishment, my brother was a hero in my eyes, waxing the fiberglass hood of his Corvette, squirting hose water at his girlfriend, a May Day Queen with a teased ball of auburn hair. He was funny and liked practical jokes; he put a live frog in the ice cream freezer at the local drugstore. Although my father had to pay for the discarded ice cream, my brother's prank became legendary, inflating his status in our hometown, and some of the glory spilled onto me.

My brother's moods changed with whiplash speed and without apparent cause, as if he were controlled by a hidden, malfunctioning switch. As a matter of survival, I learned to recognize his three, basic settings: Affable, Seething, and Homicidal. As I grew wise—say, around the age of seven—I realized I had the power to control the switch that controlled him. I used this power to exact revenge for the ball-beanings and face-squashing sessions. I tipped his mood toward Seething whenever I could. I was living dangerously, but that was half the fun.

When my brother's girlfriend joined us for dinner, I waited for her to take a bite of lasagna and announced, "The dog

RON NYSWANER

just farted." Or, once I observed to her, "Your chest is really pointy." Having been told by my brother how my "sissyish" behavior humiliated him (and my parents, my extended family, my Little League team, and all my brother's friends), I drew attention to my girlish qualities just to set him off. It was a paradox. I dreaded being called a sissy and struggled to repress all those mysterious behaviors that gave me away. But the pleasure I derived from making my brother squirm overrode my fear of derision. When one of his softball team pals came to our house, I asked him in a lilting tone, "If you could paint your room any color in the world, what color would you paint it?" My brother's eyes narrowed and he exhaled through his nostrils—a cartoon bull facing a matador—and I knew I'd pay the next time we were alone in the house. I'd get the pillow treatment; he'd squash my nose, muffle my cries, pin my flailing arms. Or I'd be sitting some afternoon in my sandbox and he'd round the corner, with one hand behind his back, counting, "One…two…" I might try to run, but the ball would find its target, catching me between my shoulder blades or smacking the back of my head. I accepted the inevitability of pain. I came to look forward to it, finding satisfaction in the contact, the attention, and the emotional intensity.

These memories were not repressed; they had not been "recovered" in therapy or through hypnosis. They simmered beneath the skin of my emotional life, surfacing at inconvenient moments, usually during sober sex. An unexpected embrace enraged me; I couldn't bear anything that threatened my breathing. I kept the episodes with my brother—what I called, mentally, my "pain training"—a secret, in the same category as slapping my own face, engaging in solitary drug abuse, banging my head against a wall, and letting my ankles burn at noon in near-equatorial sun. I nourished a deeply held belief that the key to survival was silent suffering. It was no accident that my favorite historical figure was Saint Joan of Arc.

86

Johann shot out of the pool and shook himself like a dog. "Ronnie," he said, "are you crazy? Your feet look like lobsters."

Johann and I rode to Stock Island, twenty-three miles north of Key West, in Kenny and Emmanuel's Mustang convertible, Mariah Carey blaring from the speakers. Kenny had called in the afternoon and suggested an exclusive restaurant on its own island. I accepted the invitation without consulting Johann, part of my plan to stop trying to please him, which I hoped would please him. Before leaving the guesthouse, I coated my sunburned ankles in a thick layer of cold cream and loosened the laces of my shoes. I hobbled to the car when our hosts arrived.

The Seven Mile Bridge that connects the lower Keys is slung low to the water. The fading sun made the ocean flat and metallic; the air felt thick and smelled sweet. Johann occupied two thirds of the backseat. I jimmied into the space that remained, feigning indifference yet thrilled to press my hips against his. When we pulled up to the ferry that carried passengers to the island restaurant, Johann pounded the headrest and declared, "I decide *now*—I want crème caramel for dessert! If this place does not have crème caramel, I burn it down!"

I barked at an imaginary waiter, "And put some chocolate sauce on that crème caramel!"

The restaurant was made of dark, weathered wood, surrounded by palm trees, and open to the air. The waitress was chipper and suntanned, with muscular arms and legs like a tennis pro. "Keep your eyes out for Key deer," she suggested.

Kenny and Emmanuel described Key deer while Johann examined the menu. These are deer whose growth has been stunted by the tropical vegetation of the Keys. They're exactly like the deer of the northeastern United States, with antlers and fluffy white tails, except Key deer never grow beyond the size of a German shepherd.

"Sounds bogus to me," I said, accusing Kenny and Emmanuel of joining the waitress in a conspiracy to put on gullible tourists.

Emmanuel interrogated me about my life up north, my career, my trips to Los Angeles, trying to calculate Johann's place in it all. I avoided specifics, but Emmanuel drilled for answers. Had I stayed in Johann's apartment? Had he visited me in Woodstock? What kind of music did we listen to when we were together? Did we like the same kinds of movies? Kenny offered a Southern gentleman's soft, slightly embarrassed smile, occasionally trying to change the subject but defeated by the tenacious Emmanuel.

"Now let me get this straight. You two have been dating... How long?"

I was stunned when Johann answered, "Two years." His eyes never left the menu. "I met Ronnie when I came to New York for business."

"So you get to travel for your *business*."

"All the time."

"You must meet all kinds of interesting people."

"For sure."

"Mostly men, I assume." Emmanuel stroked his brown throat and I noticed that his fingernails were varnished.

"Men, women. I do not discriminate."

"I'm a little confused. What exactly *is* your—?"

Johann interrupted. "Yes, they have it! Ronnie! Crème caramel!" He slammed the menu to the table, rattling the wineglasses. "I am ready to order! I export furniture to Europe."

I decided Emmanuel resembled a little terrier I'd had when I was a kid, a cranky, arthritic bitch with sinus problems who refused to be moved when curled into her favorite chair. "What *kind* of furniture?"

"Beautiful furniture. So beautiful you cannot believe how beautiful it is." Johann set aside his menu, resting both arms on the table, facing Emmanuel squarely.

"I met Ronnie in a bar. Do you know the Townhouse on 52nd Street? Classy place. I saw Ronnie drinking a martini. He looked so handsome I said to myself, *I must meet this man.* But he won't look at me. I think, *I have to get this man's attention.* So I take the straw from my Diet Pepsi—I never touch alcohol or drugs or coffee or cigarettes—I take the straw from my Diet Pepsi and I blow a little air through the straw in Ronnie's direction. He doesn't notice. So I roll up a little piece of paper and I spit it through the straw and I hit him right in his ear. This little piece of paper gets stuck in Ronnie's ear, but he doesn't know. So now I have to tell him he's got a little piece of paper stuck in his ear, or he will walk out of the bar and people on the street will laugh at him, you know. And maybe he has a date or a business engagement, and I don't want him to go to something important like that with a little piece of paper stuck in his ear; he looked ridiculous. So I take an ice cube from my glass of Diet Pepsi and I throw it at him, but I hit this big bodybuilder sitting next to Ronnie. I don't like to judge people, but I think maybe this bodybuilder is a prostitute, and maybe he thinks he can get Ronnie to pay for sex. So I hit this bodybuilder in the eye with my little ice cube, and he calls me an asshole. Finally, Ronnie looks at me! But now I have this big man with all these muscles to deal with, and he's off his bar stool now and he's standing in front of me and he wants to fight. So I tell him I don't want to fight him and anyway he takes too many steroids and probably his balls are little, like marbles. He says he has big balls and they hang down real low, and I say how low and he says real, real low, and he can prove it because he did a porn movie and everyone can see how big his balls are and how they hang down real low. So I say, what's the name of the porn movie and he says *Furlong,* because there are horses in it. Ronnie says, 'I love that movie—it's my favorite!' And Ronnie buys the guy a drink, and he buys me a Diet Pepsi, and we all start talking, and the guy doesn't want to fight me anymore, but now I figure I have to get Ronnie away from this hustler, because no way do I want to do a three-way with this guy. I want Ronnie all for myself. So while we talk I put my hand down Ronnie's pants and get him all hard and I whisper in his ear, 'I want to go home with you and *fuck you all night.*' And I feel Ronnie's cock and it stands straight up. And Ronnie and me, we leave together when the body-builder goes into the bathroom to take a piss."

Emmanuel was speechless, playing with the fringe on his scarf. Two nights in a row he'd gone up against the master, and two nights in a row he'd been gored. Kenny removed a hand-kerchief from an inner pocket and wiped his brow. I realized our section of the restaurant had grown quiet, and straight couples were gaping in our direction. Our chipper waitress, who had arrived at our table halfway through Johann's story, while the bodybuilder was defending the size of his balls, stood mutely at Johann's side. It seemed as if the entire restaurant's staff had halted service at this moment, as there was no clanking of flatware or scraping of plates. I heard ocean water lapping against the shore beyond the wooden deck. I saw the moon hanging in a crescent above the anchored yachts at the wharf and I felt the world stand still.

Johann had lied for me. Was this some kind of sign?

He turned to the waitress. "I want to order dessert first. And *don't* tell me you're out of crème caramel."

Ten

Dinner proceeded comfortably after Johann's X-rated monologue. Emmanuel relaxed, turned sweet and attentive toward Johann, even fawning, the way a weaker dog rolls onto its back to honor the alpha. He regaled us with tales of his childhood in Cuba and won Johann's heart by speaking lovingly of his mother and her chicarones, tamales, and stews. One understood why Kenny loved Emmanuel and forgave him his excesses and bitchiness; his life in Cuba had been dreadful and yet he had survived and thrived, and he concentrated his bitterness on campy asides and comments about the wardrobes and hairstyles of clueless heterosexuals.

Kenny told stories about their early days together, the reaction of his church to his homosexuality, the threats, the surprising moments of compassion among his redneck congregation. He spoke in his genteel voice; I imagined he must have been a fine minister, leading a Bible study or comforting a widow. Toward the end of the meal we felt friendly toward each other, connected in that "It's a small world" kind of way, stuffed with a Floridian version of nouvelle American cuisine: red snapper, shrimp, filet mignon, braised vegetables, roasted whole cloves of garlic, and finally dessert and with it, a visitor.

Johann spotted the deer first, halfway through his second crème caramel. "Oh, Ronnie," he said. "What the fuck is that?"

I saw the creature poking its muzzle through the balustrade. It was smaller than a German shepherd and carried a grand rack of antlers, four or five points. My father, a passionate deer hunter, would have been proud to mount this rack on his wall.

Kenny said, "Now that, my friends, is the famous Key deer. He's swum over from the bigger island, and I daresay he's looking for something to eat."

Johann squatted in front of the deer. Other patrons stepped close to admire the animal, but Johann claimed it for himself, obstructing the view. "Ronnie, give me my crème caramel."

I carried the dessert to Johann. He scooped a glob of custard onto his middle finger and offered it to the deer, who sniffed and stepped back. Kenny said, "He doesn't seem interested in crème caramel."

Emmanuel added, "Maybe he's lactose intolerant."

Johann responded, only for my ears, "No one turns down the master, do they, Ronnie?"

"No, sir."

The deer sniffed the air near Johann's finger with his black, wet nostrils. His tail trembled and his sides quivered. Most of the tables had emptied, and people were crowding around me and Johann and the deer. The crème caramel clung to Johann's middle finger. The deer inched closer.

I sensed everyone crowding us, felt this was as good a wedding ceremony as any, and decided—though Johann was unaware—that he would be marrying me *if* the deer accepted his creamy offering. The top-heavy creature leaned toward Johann but hesitated. Behind us, Emmanuel muttered, "I think he prefers flan."

Emmanuel's voice startled the deer, and his triangular ears went erect. I feared he would dash away, taking my imagined wedding ceremony with him into the cluster of palms and black gulf water.

Then, the deer stretched his neck another inch, until his tongue reached Johann's finger, and he licked it clean.

Later, in the restroom, I was surprised by my own reflection. I looked relaxed, suntanned, clear-eyed, and happy. It was after midnight and I was sober. Johann and I had two days left to our vacation, and I was convinced—courtesy of a tremulous, antlered messenger—that the rest of our time together would be free of binges, hangovers, and the correlated despair.

I came out of the restroom and found Johann and Emmanuel standing at the bar, speaking to an exotic, dark-skinned person of ambiguous gender, with broad shoulders, muscular, bare arms and legs, wearing a silk kimono, hair in a bun shot through with two chopsticks.

"Who's that?" I asked Kenny.

"That's Sparkle," he answered. "The biggest coke dealer in Key West."

Johann and I spent the rest of our vacation in Key West partying with Sparkle, a black, Dutch-born, twenty-four seven transvestite who made grand entrances and walked in the middle of the street. Sparkle had an abhorrence of sidewalks. "For tourists," he declared. He wore a police whistle on a chain around his neck and blew it frequently, announcing, with a wave of his big black hand, "Fashion police, you're under arrest!" He tortured overweight Midwesterners, ordering them out of the gay section of Old Town. "You there, Shamu!" he shouted. "Back to Sloppy Joe's!"

Sparkle sold lousy coke, with a sour, metallic taste that reminded me of foot powder. "It *is* foot powder, honey," he explained; it was the ingredient he used to cut his stock. The hours droned on, through a night of barhopping, an unwelcome sunrise, a suffocating afternoon spent semiconscious, and a second evening of meandering "fun." I dragged Johann along a bar crawl as Sparkle's entourage, with Sparkle rewarding us with bumps from his bitter stash. Johann grew sullen, uncomfortable as a drag queen's groupie, but neither of us seemed capable of mustering the will to turn down free drugs. I got drunk as well, on margaritas, buying rounds for Sparkle and his friends, particularly some brawny strippers, while Johann brooded over Diet Pepsis. Our vacation turned into a purgatory that wiped out everything pleasant that had come before, even memories of the totemic deer with the sweet tooth.

In predawn hours, on our last night together, I lay next to Johann in the guest room, waiting to hear him snore. I raised to an elbow. Johann stayed on his back, a sheet draped over his legs. I feared I might never lie in a bed with him again, and this fear fed my hunger as well as my courage. I slid the sheet from his hips and gazed. I caressed him below his belly button; he twitched and I stroked him, making him hard. His face revealed neither interest nor discouragement.

I squatted over him, pointing him toward me.

Johann opened his eyes. "What the fuck are you doing?"

Early in our relationship I had rejected Johann's overtures at mastering me; I enjoyed his gentleness, his protection, his warmth. But before he left me, I wanted the part he gave to others, that element of himself I believed he withheld from me.

"Ronnie. Are you crazy? Not even a condom?"

Johann slid out from under and I collapsed onto the bed, rejected and humiliated. I *never* practiced unsafe sex. What had come over me?

"What do you want, Ronnie? You want me to beat you? Fist you? Call you a piece of shit?"

"No. Maybe…"

"You don't want me to be Johann tonight? You want me to be the master?"

I didn't know what I wanted. I knew only that I didn't want Johann to sleep, to lie next to me disengaged. If he could not make love to me with genuine desire, then I wanted him to take me with the passion of anger, even paid-for, scripted anger.

"You could hold me down. You could force me. Charge me extra, anything you want. I'll write a check. You do it for everyone else."

When Johann spoke he sounded exhausted: "I think I am getting too old for my type of work."

He climbed onto the bed, all business. "Listen, Ronnie. We can have sex, okay. Don't worry that it's five in the morning and you dragged me into fourteen bars after some fucking queen with bullshit coke. I'm tired, so you can suck me. Go on." He propped a pillow against the headboard and settled onto it, legs spread. "But remember, Johann doesn't fuck and Johann doesn't get fucked."

As I serviced Johann, feeling his contempt, my arms drifted northward on the bed and Johann took the cue, wrapping his hands around my wrists, holding me in place, fulfilling the circular logic of paid-for, sexual sadism, "forcing" me to satisfy him, which is what I was paying him to do.

Crystal

Eleven

A simple illicit love affair without risk concerns mere pleasure, whereas an affair which is experienced as a "challenge to the gallows"...involves the thrill of entering a forbidden domain.

—SLAVOJ ZIZEK, *FOR THEY KNOW NOT WHAT THEY DO: ENJOYMENT AS A POLITICAL FACTOR*

NEW YORK CITY— AUGUST, 1996

I stood outside the Paramount Hotel on 46th Street and watched as Johann walked toward me, nodding to prostitutes, drag queens, mounted police, and bicycle messengers the way a country club regular nods to the staff as he enters the clubhouse: friendly, comfortable but not equitable, projecting kinship with New York's street life and superiority to it at the same time. He may have been a master in Los Angeles. But with that walk he was *the* master of New York.

He stood before me and I tried a joke. "Is that a cell phone in your pocket or are you glad to see me?"

Johann never deigned to acknowledge a joke, as if life was too absurd to laugh at anything specific. "How are you, Ronnie?"

"Great. What do we do now?" There was a room reserved for us at the Paramount Hotel, but I didn't want to seem over-anxious. The sun was, after all, still shining.

"I am sure you would like to buy me dinner."

In the weeks that followed my Key West adventure with Johann, I worked on my script about poor people, my white trash romantic comedy. A producer telephoned to pass along notes from the actress Ashley Judd, who was "circling the idea" of playing the lead. Judd had offered a tidbit from her rural childhood: a dinner scene in which children cajole a guest into trading potatoes for hunks of meat. I was instructed to "find a place" for this homely moment in my script, as if a screenplay is a communal chest of drawers where one finds "places" for the memories of actresses, like putting away underwear and socks on laundry day.

One night, Johann called to announce he was coming east to see an old friend. We arranged to meet in New York, "the city where no one sleeps," as Johann referred to it. Secretly, I hoped to entice him to travel with me to Woodstock when his personal business in New York was finished.

We had dinner in the hip restaurant on the Paramount's second floor. Johann ordered fried calamari, clam chowder, pepper-crusted filet mignon in blue cheese sauce, garlic mashed potatoes, Diet Pepsi, and a pear tart with chocolate ice cream. The chef did not intend the tart to be served with ice cream, so there was a brouhaha about it between Johann and the waitress. Johann settled the matter by speaking in a foreign language (German, I assumed, as he had told me he was German) to a busboy who conveyed something to the maître d', who approached our table and said, in an accent as vague as Johann's, "No problem."

My covert plan involved a fantasy: Once Johann bedded down in my house in Woodstock he would never leave. He would be seduced by my gardens; my three huge, licking dogs; the clean air; the mountains; the stream in my back-yard. I lived, after all, in a Catskills version of the Garden of

Eden. But, like the God of Creation, I was lonely and desired a companion. I would make Johann from the dust of my need.

"I have a surprise for you," he said, adding whipped cream to the pear tart (the whipped cream had appeared after another dramatic encounter between Johann and the staff).

"And I have one for you," I answered, thinking of my plans. I wondered if Johann had ever ventured to the top of the Empire State Building at night. It seemed a romantic spot for a proposal. But first, to broach the subject: "How long are you staying in New York?"

Licking his fork, Johann answered, "Just a few days. Then I go to Fire Island with my friend."

"Who is this friend?" We were in our hotel room, with Johann sitting on the edge of bed, unfolding foil packets.

"Ethan? I know him from the days I lived in New York. He is sophisticated, like you, Ronnie, and smart. He listens all the time to classical music. This is the only problem I have with him, classical music all the time. I go crazy. He takes me to Fire Island every summer."

Johann's obvious affection for Ethan put me into a combative mood. "Is he a friend? Or a client?" I split the word into two, aggressively accented syllables, "cli-*ent*."

"What's the difference?"

"Indeed."

Johann slapped both hands against his face. "This is what I get for trying to make everybody happy. Ronnie, forget about Ethan. He sends me big packages full of Mozart CD's. You think I want to listen to Mozart twenty-four hours a day? Come here. I bring you something special, all the way from L.A."

On the nightstand, Johann arranged four plump dashes of pinkish-yellow powder. "What's with the itty-bitty, little lines?"

"Try it."

I preferred to pout. "Why don't you let me meet Ethan? We can have dinner, the three of us."

"Maybe." It was a "maybe" that meant never.

"What's the matter? Are you ashamed of me?"

"Right," Johann said. "I'm ashamed of the guy who wins an Oscar for writing *Philadelphia*. I don't want to be seen with him. Ronnie, what's the matter with you?"

"I didn't win. I was nominated." I massaged Johann's shoulders while he rolled a twenty-dollar bill into a tube.

"You snort a little, Ronnie. Go slow. This is not coke. This is better. You're going to tweak tonight."

"I suppose Ethan doesn't take drugs."

"No," Johann smiled. "He's addicted to me."

I hovered above the miniature lines. Was this a test? Ethan consumed Johann sober, while I needed to be high. I wondered how Johann would react if I swatted the drugs from the table and dove between his legs with undiluted desire. Would I be elevated to Ethan's status, a "friend?"

Johann waited for me to do one thing or the other, wearing a blank (just this side of bored) expression. It was always like this with Johann: So many moments seemed to be *the* moment. It was exhausting. How could anyone navigate this road of distance and desire *without* drugs? And a new drug offered new possibilities, new dreams, new potential to find the courage required to escort Johann into my life. A universe of possibilities rested in that jot of piss-colored dust.

I bent toward the table with the rolled-up twenty positioned at my nostril. I chose not to look at Johann. I didn't want to see the knowing look he assumed whenever I did exactly what he expected me to do. True, I was predictable. But so was he. I held the position that everything mattered while he held the position that nothing mattered. We were well-matched: the sucker and the cynic, a postmodern vaudeville act.

I snorted a bump. It smacked the back of my throat with

little effect, although the taste was acrid and sickening, like oven cleaner. "I don't feel anything."

"You wait. It's slower than coke. It sneaks up on you. Ronnie? Are you going to calm down tonight, or do I have to tie you up and fuck you with a dildo?"

"That'll be the—" I stopped speaking. Rather, my speaking was stopped, by a geyser of warmth and pleasure that started at the base of my neck and expanded around my skull to my ears, my cheeks, and my forehead. The physical sensation was accompanied by a deep feeling of satisfaction, near-euphoria and then, with a jolt, my groin tingled and I felt as if I was having sex, even though I was standing in the middle of the room, fully dressed, not being touched by anyone nor touching myself. It felt as if I was the center of an orgy and all the invisible participants were working overtime to satisfy me.

"You're tweak-ing." Johann singsonged his words.

"What...is...this...stuff?"

"What's the matter? You never do crystal before?" Johann unzipped his pants. "Poor Ronnie. I have to teach you everything."

Johann taught me everything he knew about crystal meth. It's made from ephedrine, the main ingredient in Sudafed, combined with red phosphorous, hydrochloric acid, and other chemicals distilled from household products such as lye, drain cleaner, lantern fuel, and...

Johann paused, searching for words. "What's that stuff you put in your car, in the winter?"

"*Antifreeze?*"

"Right."

"How do you know so much about this stuff?"

"I went to a seminar at UCLA." Johann stood at the window, peering through metal blinds to harsh daylight. We had been inside the room for fifteen hours, doing nothing but snorting crystal, having sex, and talking about snorting crystal and having

103

sex. Sometimes we talked about talking. I asked questions: "Do you think I'm talking too much?" Johann answered: "Ronnie, don't ask me questions all the time." The world had shrunk, as constrained as our room, where you had to navigate the pseudo-1970s molded plastic chairs to get to the bathroom.

Johann walked around naked. He jerked his cock persistently but absentmindedly, the way some people rattle change in their pockets. I spent a great deal of time putting on my socks and taking them off.

Johann and I careered through a menu of crystal's side effects. I alternated between sleepiness and alertness, when the sights and sounds of our room shifted from foggy to clear, the way letters change during an eye exam as a stronger lens replaces a weaker one. I seemed to awaken at intervals, hearing the click of the digital clock on the VCR as the minutes crept forward. I veered from a feeling of being completely alone—not merely in the room, but in the universe, floating in a *Star Trek*–inspired vortex, empty and at peace—to an oppressive awareness of every one of Johann's movements, people laughing in the streets, taxicab engines idling, the ding of the elevator at the end of the hall.

Johann's high seemed tinged with paranoia. He was sweating. He stood at the window, deciding whether the Venetian blinds—another of the room's retro-style touches—blocked more light if tilted up or down. He approached the problem scientifically; he tugged the cord to tilt them up, stood back and studied the effect. He tugged the cord and twisted them down, stood back and studied the effect. He tugged the cord and twisted them…

"Does it look stupid for me to wear socks when I'm naked? My feet are cold, but I think it looks stupid."

Johann ignored me, concentrating on something glimpsed out the window. "What are those guys doing on the roof?"

"Do they look like construction workers?"

"Yeah."

"Maybe they're construction workers."

"But what are they doing on the *roof?*"

"Johann. Come lie beside me."

The most fantastic thing happened: Johann obeyed. He stretched over the bleached sheets, on his back. I stayed on my side; I knew better than to try to hold him. But I stroked his forearm with my fingers. Each of us played with ourselves, one of crystal's side effects: obsessive masturbation to the point of calluses. But somehow it seemed natural, even cozy. And in our bizarre approximation of the intimate conversation of lovers, we exchanged stories of our "first times." Not our first times having sex. Our first encounters with paid-for sex.

Johann told me about the man who stared at him while he was walking along a Berlin street. This was long before he came to America and discovered hustler bars. He had been strolling near the train station when the man looked him over. They went to a one-star hotel near the station and the man paid Johann for fifteen minutes of sex, asking Johann to do nothing, merely to stand there. The event puzzled Johann, but he had a good meal on the man's money, at an outdoor restaurant where they played disco music. As Johann was eating, the man walked by. His eyes met Johann's, but he continued walking, heading down an alley where Johann had heard that other boys—desperately poor straight boys with lice, mostly from Romania—waited to be picked up by men like the one who had paid Johann and now ignored him. Johann wouldn't have minded having dinner with the man and practicing his Italian, but the man no longer was interested in Johann. Johann was old news.

"Italian?" I asked. "I thought you were in Berlin."

"He was a tourist," Johann snapped. "This is when I start to figure them out."

"Who?" *Tourists?*

"Men who buy boys."

I said nothing about the several hundred dollars I'd given him at the start of the evening.

"Some of these guys, it's like a safari. They're always hunting. First they get a rabbit. Then they want a tiger. Then they want a lion. Or they want a rabbit again, but a different one. They had a black rabbit. Now they want a white rabbit. Something different all the time."

"Not always."

Johann changed the subject. "Your turn."

I told Johann about Chris Thompson, whom I'd found through an ad in a gay magazine during a business trip to Los Angeles. The ads were brazen (*"Playgirl* centerfold, *GQ* handsome, lots of muscles, and ten thick inches") and promised so much pleasure ("Tattooed, uncut surfer dude loves to party") that I read them compulsively, in my hotel room, after a day of meetings, where I negotiated changes on screenplays in "development." Script development involves months and years of writing and rewriting with the likely outcome of there being *no* outcome, as most scripts are shelved. The "escort" ads guaranteed an outcome, literally ("I will make you explode!"). After a day in the purgatory of feature film development, I couldn't resist.

Chris Thompson lived in the hills above Sunset Boulevard in a house that was all carpet and mirrors with no furniture, at least none in the living room, the only room I was allowed to enter. I had seen Chris in a porn movie called *Deep Shaft*, in which he played a coal miner. I assumed he was playing a coal miner, although he remained prone on a sofa-bed. Halfway through his scene he put on a hard hat and referred to his penis as his "deep shaft," as if someone had realized they needed to do something to justify the movie's title.

Chris Thompson was one of the most beautiful men I'd ever met. His muscles were heavy and his legs were thick; his skin was bronze and his teeth were white. He answered the door wearing a towel, yawning, and settled onto the carpet in the middle of the room. He did nothing to encourage me to touch him; he certainly did not touch me. He opened his hand for my money and, when I handed it to him, counted it with the deftness of a croupier. He leaned on his elbows—my cue, I assumed, to enjoy myself. My hands were cold and he told me so. I sallied forth and managed to make him hard when he said, "You don't want me to come, do you? I've already had three orgasms today."

Johann interjected: "What a lousy prostitute."

I pressed forward with my story. I assured Chris that an orgasm wasn't required and that I too was sleepy and maybe we should just talk. He seemed relieved and became a gracious host, pouring me a drink and making chitchat. When I told Chris I lived in Ulster County, New York, near the Ashokan Reservoir, he became animated. He was a student of alien sightings and particularly fond of the books of Ulster County resident Whitley Strieber, who wrote the alien abduction manifesto, *Communion*. Chris told me how the Ashokan Reservoir—my local landmark and a source for New York City's drinking water—was a beacon to interstellar navigators.

"What a nut," Johann said.

Chris believed he was a lifelong, multiple abductee and soon would be transported to another galaxy. While we talked he remained naked, and I tried not to stare at his "deep shaft," which flopped about as he described the sessions of hypnosis that had revealed his life as the subject of interplanetary experimentation. Finally, Chris apologized for talking so much, explaining he'd taken four hits of ecstasy and added—quickly—that he was sorry but he didn't have any X for me, although he could, as a way of making amends, give me the number of his ecstasy dealer, a legally blind guy named Mel.

Johann crowed, "I know him!"

"Chris?"

"No, Mel! Old guy, right? His apartment is full of books. Books everywhere."

"He used to be in publishing, before he went blind. That's why he sells ecstasy."

"Ronnie! What a small world, huh? We have the same dealer for X! You know, that guy Chris ripped you off. I hope you acted like a man and got your money back."

"I enjoyed myself."

Johann shook his head, disappointed. "Ronnie. You are too nice. You forget the most important rule: A hustler is a hustler."

The room dropped into silence, tense with too much information. Johann rescued the moment. "I promise. If I ever run into this guy, I'll get your money for you. With interest. And the next time you come to L.A., you can forget about these people. I'll get you ecstasy."

I leaned forward and kissed Johann on the neck, then moved my mouth lower, to his shoulder, chest, and belly. There were vague questions floating in my mind regarding the contradictions in Johann's stories, but they faded with my licking and sucking. I replaced the questions with a single word, the last word he had spoken before I began to service him; it seeped through my pores, repeating itself with every beat of blood at my temple and in my cock.

Ecstasy.

Twelve

Volatile gases are released during the boiling of the mixture, which are fatal if inhaled and may result in an explosion. Apartment preparation is not recommended.

—INTERNET RECIPE FOR CRYSTAL METH

Crystal meth—also known as speed, crank, glass, ice, chalk, zip, and cristy—appears on the street as pale yellow lumps of moist powder, which, when snorted, ingested, smoked, or injected, stimulate the central nervous system. Several hours, even days, of euphoria and increased alertness are followed by paranoia, irritability, anxiety, insomnia, tremors, confusion, flailing movements, visual and auditory hallucinations, delusions of parasites on the skin, suicidal or homicidal thoughts, hypertension, accelerated heartbeat, elevated blood pressure, irreversible damage to the blood vessels in the brain, and cardiovascular collapse. There are also corollary, behavioral side effects that include incessant talking and teeth grinding. These last two symptoms alternate, as it is impossible to talk and grind your teeth at the same time. Teeth grinding is, of course, incompatible with certain types of sexual behavior.

Considering the level of paranoia and debilitation that accompany the use of crystal, the options for activity are limited. Dancing, having sex, talking about sex, thinking about having sex, asking other people to have sex, watching other people have sex, and watching porn videos work; thinking, eating, sleeping do not. Staring into space and weeping are alternatives. Jokes are made about the fastidiously clean houses of "tweakers" who vacuum for hours on end. (I have been inside the apartments of tweakers and crank dealers, and *fastidious* and *vacuum cleaner* are not words that come to mind.)

Some people have been known to stay awake on crystal for epic duration; the record, according to the self-styled champ who spoke at Johann's seminar, is 16 days.

"My neighborhood is the tweaking capital of the world!" Johann declared with civic pride. "Walk around West Hollywood in the morning. The guys come out, walking their dogs, no shirts, just these little shorts, with big hard-ons. Everyone's looking at everyone else, trying to pick someone up. Sometimes three or four of them go home together."

"What do they do with the dogs?" I asked.

In 1982, I saw gay West Hollywood for the first time with my first agent, Ira, who waved at the stucco houses and art deco apartment buildings from the driver's seat of his Mercedes and said, "Welcome to the Swish Alps." A fire engine crossed our path, and Ira cut a left through a red light, behind the truck. "Let's chase it! The last time I chased a fire truck it was Cesar Romero's house. I watched the damn thing burn down, all the way to the begonias."

I had sold a script to the director Jonathan Demme, who sold it to the Ladd Company, and I took on Jonathan's agent, Ira, who represented Bette Midler. I rode from the airport to the agency's headquarters in my first limousine.

I walked into Ira's office. He remained behind his desk, on the telephone. There was a poster from Bette Midler's movie *The Rose* on the wall. Ira declaimed into the telephone, "We pass on that offer, my friend. *Pass. Pasadena.*" He nodded to a long-haired assistant who approached me, digging into a little brown bottle with a tiny spoon. She placed a spoonful of coke under my nose—it was an *Alice in Wonderland* miniature silver spoon, with a filigreed handle—and I snorted.

Ira hung up and sighed. "Don't these clowns know I've lost my tolerance for these Hollywood games? Ever since Natalie died…" He snorted some coke. "Did you know Natalie Wood lived in fear, absolute *fear*, of drowning? And that's how she died, of course. Is that too incomprehensible? She was my best friend. I can't tell you how much her loss has affected me. Not to mention the loss to this industry. And cinema, in general. What's your favorite Natalie Wood movie?"

"*Inside Daisy Clover!*" I shouted, as my sinus passages caught on fire and my brain left my head, zooming toward the ceiling.

Ira nodded, mournfully. "The scene in the sound booth…"

"The scene in the sound booth!" I began singing the number from *Inside Daisy Clover* that Natalie sings as she decompensates into a nervous breakdown: "The circus is a wacky world, how I love it!" Ira joined me. We merely repeated this line, as it was—apparently—the only one we knew. He pointed at me and proclaimed to his assistant, who was scraping the bottom of the brown bottle for the last of the coke, "I knew I did the right thing taking on this kid! He's great. Isn't he great?"

At this moment a large woman with a phalanx of sun-damaged, streaked hair, wearing a muumuu and no shoes, waddled into the room. I thought she might be some insane homeless person who'd gotten past security, or a pathetic cleaning lady kept on the payroll out of pity. "This is Beth Grossman," Ira said, introducing me to the most famous agent in the world.

Beth Grossman shook my hand so hard it nearly fell off. "Wonderful," she barked. "You're great. Really talented. I think I read one of your scripts. What was the name of it? It doesn't matter. I probably didn't get a chance to read it. But I will, someday. Who knows? You're going to be rich and famous just like Bo Goldman." And she waddled out of the room.

"She seems nice," I said to Ira.

"She's a cunt," he replied. "Want a quaalude?"

At Ira's house, televisions played in every room. "I'm a media person," he explained. We dressed for an awards dinner. Ira sized me up. "Don't know how I feel about the beard and the acrylic sweater. Kind of Pittsburgh."

"I'm *from* Pittsburgh," I protested.

"You're in Beverly Hills now, baby."

I asked the housekeeper for a pair of scissors. I attacked my beard in the guest bathroom. Ira seemed pleased when I emerged, without the sweater and clean-shaven.

"I knew you were going to do that." He was smoking a joint. He asked me what I liked to drink.

"Jack Daniel's on the rocks."

"For God's sake, Ernest Hemingway." Ira said. "I hope you're not going to light a pipe."

The quaalude I'd swallowed an hour earlier took hold of my brain, plunging me into a dreamy state; I felt as if I had dived into a pool of warm water. Ira's words floated toward me, and some of them became disconnected from the others. Ira found me standing in his bedroom, staring at a photograph of Barbra Streisand sitting on his lap. His hair had been longer then, a big, bushy head of hair. "Look at me with my Jew-fro," he said, putting a drink into my hand.

I stared at my drink, fascinated with the ice clinking musically against etched glass. The plinking of the ice was musical. I opened my mouth to thank Ira for the drink but realized I had lost the ability to speak. I remained calm; perhaps God had taken away my speech that I might develop other abilities. The ability to listen, for example, so crucial for a writer. I saw myself doing interviews, the famous writer who did not speak. Of course, the interviews would be short and one-sided. I would scrawl my answers on a pad or make use of my favorite childhood toy, an Etch A Sketch. I wondered how I might meet

Barbra Streisand and if she would sit on my lap. I wondered if she would be heavy. I wondered if she would find it strange or endearing that I wasn't able to speak.

Ira snatched the bourbon from my hand. "Water for you, Miss Pittsburgh. And no more vitamin Q's."

I remained silent during the drive to the Beverly Hills Hotel, which suited Ira fine, as he liked to play pop music at the loudest possible volume. At dinner I was relegated, with Ira's assistant, to a table near the kitchen. But we joined Ira for dessert at the main table, while waiting for his client Bette Midler to receive an Entertainer of the Year award. The award was going to be presented by the previous year's recipient, Liberace. During the opening festivities, Bette sat across the table from me with Liberace nearby; I brushed elbows with his "chauffeur," Scott Thorson. I began to come down from the coke and the quaalude, regaining the ability to speak. This turned out to be unfortunate, as my first words were directed in a loud voice to Bette Midler: "Isn't it funny that you and Liberace look exactly alike?"

Ira decided on the way home to chase a fire truck, but we lost it somewhere in Laurel Canyon. He pulled over and stepped out of the car, ordering me to trade places. I was willing to do anything Ira asked, considering I had insulted his most famous client. I settled into the driver's seat while Ira dug into the glove compartment, retrieving a brown vial and a compact mirror.

"Drive," he commanded.

"Where?"

"Anywhere but over a cliff. And don't hit the brakes too hard. In fact, don't worry about the brakes. Just drive."

I obeyed. It was difficult to ignore the brakes as we descended Laurel Canyon toward Hollywood, for the road was steep and meandering. I put the Mercedes into third gear and kept it there.

"How much did this car cost?"

Ira was bent over the mirror, chopping lines. "Forty."

"Whew," I whistled. "How much am I getting for my script?"

"Twenty-five against a hundred."

"Whew," I whistled again.

Ira snorted a bump so hard he might have sucked up the mirror along with the coke. He held a rolled-up hundred-dollar bill under my nose. I took one hand from the steering wheel, to hold down one of my nostrils, and snorted. Ira waxed reflective.

"Hey," he said. "I haven't corrupted you, have I?"

The road dropped into a steep decline and I needed to brake. But I was aware of the bumps of coke on the mirror in Ira's hand. He held the round mirror with his fingertips, the way I had been trained as a waiter to hold a tray of cocktails. I downshifted to second. The car's motor began to grind, but Ira didn't notice.

"You've done drugs before, right? My God, you're what? Twenty-five years old? I mean, I'm not like some kind of corrupting influence, am I? I'm not some kind of Houdini?"

"I think you mean Svengali." I was aware of a feeling of power. "I'm twenty-one."

"Twenty-*one*?"

I shifted up to third and touched the gas. We squealed around a turn on the edge of a crevasse, and I saw the lights of downtown Los Angeles. "I'm a coke virgin," I admitted. "And a quaalude virgin. And a Mercedes virgin." I shifted into fourth and let loose on the stretch that connects Laurel Canyon to Fountain Avenue.

Ira was writhing. "I'm so sick," he cried. "I'm a corrupter. It's this business. It's an infection. It's pervasive." His voice became low and mournful. "*This fucking business killed Natalie Wood.*"

Each of us was silent for a few seconds, in honor of Natalie. Then we burst into song: "The circus is a wacky world, how I love it!"

But Ira stopped short. "What's that smell?" He wrinkled his nose. "What the hell have you done to my car?"

A knock on the hotel room door propelled Johann—teetering on the edge of paranoia—into the bathroom. It was a housekeeper, ignoring the "Do Not Disturb" sign.

"No service, please.

"You no want towels?"

From the bathroom: "No towels, Ronnie!"

"No, thank you! We're fine!"

The housekeeper rapped on the door with something other than her knuckles, something with a metallic sound; I pictured the barrel of a handgun. Her voice emanated only a few inches above the door knob. "Open the do-o-or, I give you tow-wels."

I stood outside the bathroom, respecting Johann's privacy. "I think we ought to take the towels. Then she'll go away."

With utter terror Johann said, "She's a midget."

"She's not a midget. She's Hispanic."

"Okay, okay, Ronnie," Johann snapped. "Take the towels if you think it's so important."

I took plush, fresh towels from a smiling Puerto Rican maid, and Johann stayed in the bathroom for the next hour. I never heard him turn on a spigot or flush the toilet.

The illusion of crystal is that there is no hard crash. When we reached the end of our stash, we ventured out of the Paramount Hotel to eat hamburgers at the Howard Johnson's on Broadway. I was amazed that I could eat, impossible after a coke binge. When we finished the meal, we strolled the neighborhood. Johann's paranoia had lifted; he was jaunty, touring his former stomping grounds. I remarked on this fantastic quality of crystal. We'd been taking the drug for nearly two days, and there were no ramifications. It had been a trip of euphoria, giddiness, and haziness punctuated with moments of überclarity and supersonic sexual arousal. No tremors. No self-recrimination. I walked through the world like a normal person. A very sexy normal person. A normal person who had grown a ten-inch penis overnight.

"It was bigger than normal, wasn't it? I mean, you noticed it, right? I'm not imagining it."

"Yeah, Ronnie, for sure. You're sexy. Maybe you should lower your voice."

I was silent, mustering courage to invite Johann to Woodstock. My drug-addled brain remembered something about a plan involving the top of the Empire State Building, a romantic proposal that had been misplaced during hours of sex and taking my socks on and off.

Before I could broach the subject, Johann spotted a paunchy Spanish man on Ninth Avenue feeding potato chips to a Chihuahua. "I used to buy coke from that guy. Two, three years ago. But I am sure he will know me. New York will never forget Johann." I wondered how the rest of New York would feel being represented by an unshaven man in a sweat-stained T-shirt letting a Chihuahua lick salt from his fingertips.

"I've got to get home. I have to feed my dogs. I want you to come with me. I wanted to do this on top of the Empire State Building, but…"

Johann crossed his arms. We were blocking the sidewalk, facing each other. I stared at his boots. Johann had me in that gaze of his—the figuring-things-out look, the adding-and-subtracting, what-do-you-really-want, what's-in-it-for-me look. He could stare without blinking, like a lizard.

"You want me to come to your house?"

It sounded frightening the way he said house. As if I had invited him to my dungeon, my snake pit, my hellhole. I wondered if I had finally crossed the line with Johann, the one that marked what was business and what was personal and therefore off-limits. Across the street the Spanish drug dealer's

Chihuahua danced on hind legs for another potato chip, and I saw myself as that dog, begging Johann to toss me a potato chip. *Just one more.*

I retreated to the language of paid-for sex: "I want you for an overnight."

Johann threw a leather-clad arm around my shoulders. "Ronnie, it's a great idea. Super. I want to see where you live. For sure. Do you have any trees?"

Thirteen

Finally we crashed—full throttle, a blunt collision with reality, acrid and nauseating.

Johann curled into a ball in the back of the hired car, taking us from New York to my home. "I'm sorry, Ronnie," he said. "This is not what you pay me for, but I have to sleep." I wondered what the driver made of Johann's announcement.

Our crystal crash had started as we checked out and stood outside the hotel, waiting for the car. The sun-blazed life on 46th Street had acquired a tinny, grating quality; every sound was too loud to the point of physical pain. In the car, with Johann pretending to sleep next to me, wiping me out of his consciousness with clamped-shut eyes, I sighed repeatedly and shook my head, answering a question no one had asked.

As the mile markers on the New York State Thruway whizzed by, I considered when they would end, that is, the binges and hangovers. What intervention will be necessary short of death? This thought was a frequent, unwelcome companion during periods of recuperation; I chewed on it like a soggy toothpick. At these times, my mind took on a split personality, comprising both halves of a sadomasochistic relationship. My Inner Sadist posed questions whose answers were bound to hurt, while my Inner Masochist pretended to retreat from the questions but in the end offered self-wounding answers. It went something like this:

Inner Sadist: How long have you been snorting coke?
Inner Masochist: Don't answer that question!

119

Inner Sadist: Five years?
Inner Masochist: Think about something else! Read the
names on the exit signs. Bear Mountain, Storm King…
Inner Sadist: Ten years?
Inner Masochist: Well, I remember a few binges when I lived
in the Village, and that was… Please don't make me say it!
Inner Sadist: Say what, you piece of filth?
Inner Masochist: 1986!

And so on. My Inner Sadist always won—game, set, and
match. I had to face the facts: This party I'd been throwing for
myself had lasted nearly a decade and progressed around the
world, crossing more time zones than an international cruise
ship. I calculated I had purchased illegal drugs in twenty cities,
five states, nine countries, four continents, the District of
Columbia, and Puerto Rico. I'd followed coke dealers down
shadowy alleys from Poughkeepsie to San Francisco to
Atlanta. I was nearly arrested on 13th Street in Philadelphia,
during the shooting of *Philadelphia,* when undercover cops
jumped on a dealer seconds after he'd placed two foil packets
in my hand. For some reason the cops let me walk away. In
Madrid, I shared a couple of grams of "disco dust" with a muscular, bald deaf-mute and his pudgy friend named Paco in
their cramped Volvo. Paco wrestled with me in the backseat
while the deaf-mute raced toward the Madrid suburbs, driving so fast we left the ground when the car crested a hill. Paco
kept screaming at the deaf-mute to slow down because he was
going to kill us all, and I kept screaming at Paco that there was
no point screaming at a deaf-mute. In San José, Costa Rica, I
snorted blow in the back of a taxi with a swarthy hunk named
Aldo, who fed bumps to the driver from the end of a silver key.
I was offered "smoke" or "sniff" by a dealer in Mérida, Mexico,
who worked out of his family's luggage store and insisted his
name was Samsonite, like the sign above the store. I ventured
into the favelas of Rio de Janeiro with a prostitute to cop

name was Samsonite, like the sign above the store. I ventured into the favelas of Rio de Janeiro with a prostitute to cop "coca" from men holding rifles and watched, fascinated and mystified at first, as my rented companion returned to the taxi with the stash in hand, opened his pants, and tucked the packets beneath the foreskin of his penis, assuring me it's the last place the police look.

And I tasted crystal meth for the first time in the Paramount Hotel on 46th Street in Manhattan, one August night with Johann.

"Ronnie. Where the hell are we?"

Johann brushed sleep from his eyes. His hair stuck up in the back. He looked about ten years old.

"We're home, Johann."

I paid the driver and stumbled into the house before Johann. I was a mess. My intestines were twisted in a knot and my coordination was off; I couldn't hold on to anything. There was a recurring seizing of the muscles in my right foot and a fluttering of my hands, as if I were shaking off water. Each time I made the gesture I vowed never to do it again, but thirty seconds later my hands began to tingle and then to flutter.

Johann opened the refrigerator. I warned him, "There's nothing in there but gin and sour milk." Johann went to work while I slumped at the kitchen table, sighing and shaking. I heard him open jars; something popped out of the toaster. Soon he presented me with a sandwich. I tasted olives, ketchup, and cheese on crispy bread, a bit of turkey, mayonnaise, and butter. "This is the most delicious thing I've ever eaten," I declared, truthfully. "*Ever.*"

Johann filled a tumbler with water. "I want you to drink five glasses of water before you go to bed." I didn't protest.

"I like your house, Ronnie."

"It's funky. Not some mansion. Not what you expected,

right?"

"Oh, yes, exactly what I thought," he said, handing me my second glass of water. "It looks just like Ronnie's house."

He gazed out the window, across my lavender garden to the barn. I remembered his description of his neighborhood, with tweaking studs trolling the streets for sex. It occurred to me that each of these habitats—my sixteen acres and Johann's few blocks—constituted someone's version of paradise. He allowed cold water to run from the spigot for half a minute.

I couldn't stand the way he suddenly turned silent, removing himself from the scene. I wanted him to take care of me, to bring me a glass of water. "This crash... This is one of the worst ever..."

When he spoke, there was ice in his voice. "What do you expect, Ronnie? You know what you put into your body? Something made of seven different poisons. Each one of them can kill you on its own. But someone mixes them together in just the right proportions, and they don't kill you. But you don't know who mixes them together. You don't know who cooks them and cuts them. Maybe they put in more of this, less of that. So you get some of the poison. Now your body tells you, this is how it feels when you put in poison. Why do you cry about it? If you're going to play, you have to pay."

"But *you* sold me the drugs. And I know you."

Johann filled the tumbler and carried it to me. He forced a smile and put on the master's voice: "Drink this water, you piece of shit."

"We'll never do crystal again, right?" My fingers were beginning to tingle. That queasy feeling was forming at the base of my spine, and I knew that in a few seconds I'd be flicking my hands, like my Labrador retriever shaking off pond water when she emerged from my quarry.

"I told you, Ronnie. *I* don't like drugs. I just do them to make you happy."

Johann shrieked from the bathroom when a spider crawled over his foot. "Ronnie, why didn't you tell me you had spiders?" "Wait till you see the snakes." My fantasies regarding Johann coming to live with me were being squashed—like the poor spider—as Johann faced the realities of country living. When I wanted him to leave the house, I had to park my car as close to the door as possible; he was reluctant to touch foot on grass, gravel, or soil.

"How can you live with spiders and snakes all over the place like the rain forest?"

We went to a party given by a local restaurateur named Adam. I was one of his regular customers, eating and drinking at his bar several nights a week. Often, I caused a commotion at the bar's closing, when well-intentioned patrons tried to convince me to hand over my car keys and take a taxi home. They never succeeded, but I savored the drama. This group of barflies had become my social set, as I sought the company of people who liked to drink more than they liked to do anything else. I strove to remain an outsider within my new clique and employed successful strategies toward this end; for example, I never managed to remember their names.

At Adam's wooded estate, I introduced Johann to everyone in a single stroke, "Hey, this is Johann." He said nothing. Each of us was achy and disengaged, and our sullenness threw a cloud over the festivities. Johann clomped around the blue stone deck in his thick-soled boots, glaring at the men who studied him uneasily from the pool. A valiant guest tried to reinvigorate the conversation, commenting on a piece in *The New York Times* about the slums of Rio de Janeiro. I flew into a tirade when he claimed the police were handling the situation as well as they could.

"Have you *been* to Rio?" I bellowed, startling the man as he dipped a slice of red pepper into goat cheese dip. Even Johann turned toward me, surprised by my outburst. "I have.

I've been to Rio. Do you know how the Brazilian police handle the problem of the children who live in the favela?" I had everyone's attention, including that of my stunned host, holding a burger on a metal spatula above the charcoal grill. I felt awful; I couldn't rid myself of the residual crystal meth tingling in my extremities and the smell of oven cleaner in my sinuses. "The police drive into the favela with machine guns and start shooting. They exterminate children the way we exterminate rodents. Do you think children ought to be exterminated like rodents? Adolf Hitler had similar ideas, you know."

If you ever need to stop a party dead cold, try telling someone who happens to be Jewish that his ideas are similar to Hitler's. No one spoke. My host dropped the burger to the grill and closed the lid, as if unable to look at seared meat at such a moment. Even the guests cowering in the pool, trying to avoid Johann's glare, stood frozen, with only the water making a sound, lapping against the blue stone deck.

Johann broke the silence. "I think maybe you have snakes in your pool."

Johann and I drove away from the party laughing so hard I nearly ran over some rhododendrons. In the rearview mirror I spotted my host and his guests tiptoeing along the edge of the pool, examining the bottom for snakes. The men who had been treading water when Johann made his observation had scrambled out of the pool so quickly that one of them knocked over a pitcher of piña coladas.

"Thank you, Ronnie, for the really fun party."

"You see my problem? I don't fit in. Not with them. Not with my straight friends and their kids. Not with my friends in the movie business…"

"You will always have me."

My heart flew into my throat, and for a moment I forgot I was driving. "And your mother," Johann continued. "As long as you have your mother, you know someone on earth loves you."

"But you don't have *your* mother."

"No," Johann said, checking his pager, which, as far as I could tell, hadn't beeped. "I only have myself."

From the pool party we traveled a few miles to the home of my frequently depressed carpenter friend, Armand, and his elegant Parisian wife, Caroline, who lived on a farm at the base of the Shawangunk Mountains. We had been invited for dinner to celebrate Bastille Day. Caroline's niece was visiting from Paris: Pauline, a forlorn girl of nineteen with pale skin, who sat at the table with her shoulders slumped, fondling the flatware.

Armand and Caroline received Johann and me as a legitimate couple. We had a tour of their farm, where they collected exotic fowl: black and white doves called "nuns," luminescent greenish-black Indonesian ducks, and golden long-tailed Chinese pheasants. Johann treaded stiffly across the farmyard, trying to avoid slimy clumps of duck shit, canvassing the grass before proceeding in his boots. He regarded the ramshackle farm buildings with critical eyes, while Caroline described each group of birds, first in English and then French for her niece.

"Do they *sell* these birds?" he whispered to me, following Caroline into a room with an incubator.

"No. They collect them. They like to look at them."

He disagreed. "I am sure they sell them. Or they eat them."

"They don't eat them. They just live with them."

"*Why?*"

"It makes them happy."

Caroline led us into a low-ceilinged room with chicken-wire pens. She cautioned us to enter quietly, pointing to a cubbyhole where a black pigeon nested with two gray chicks. "The father sits from ten in the morning to four in the afternoon, then the mother takes over. It's amazing, their schedule. You

125

can set your watch by it."

The father pigeon eyed us skeptically, while the chicks dozed, their fuzzy chests pulsing. Pauline lost her shyness in the presence of the chicks, exclaiming, "Adorable!"

Johann peered at the birds, then sized up Armand and Caroline, taking note of their proud smiles. "It's like you are the grandparents."

"Sort of," replied Caroline.

"They are your family," Johann insisted.

"Exactly," answered Armand.

Johann turned to me. "Now I understand."

Dinner followed in a rustic kitchen, with the doors open to summer air and mosquitoes. Caroline was a fine cook, and her grilled steak, pommes frites, and tarte tatin purged the remnants of my crystal hangover. Johann elucidated, for my sake, the tradition of Bastille Day.

"Ronnie. They pulled down the walls of the prison, so everyone could be free, all the criminals, bank robbers, murderers...even prostitutes!" He squeezed my knee beneath the table.

Pulling out of the driveway, with Caroline, Armand, and Pauline waving from the yard, with a flock of hungry geese surrounding them, I asked Johann if he had enjoyed himself. Evening had fallen, and the sky was quickening to a steely blue, with a shimmering quality, like porcelain, while the apple trees to our right and left were silhouettes, brandishing knotty limbs from hard pruning. Johann's voice, when he answered, was distant, nearly monotone, low and funereal while his words were barely accented, as if escaping from some part of himself that resisted editing.

"How many days in a year do you think I get to be a normal person?"

Fourteen

The night turned chilly. Johann and I lay in my bed, beneath a quilt made by my grandmother Leota, my father's mother, with the sewn-shut eye.

The visit with my fowl-collecting friends, perhaps the sight of the father pigeon and his progeny, inspired Johann to speak of his youth, of *his* family: stable, middle-class people (dentist mother, engineer father) with limited aspirations but the best of intentions.

Johann never meant to leave them, particularly his mother, until he met a young man on his high school ski team who became his first lover. This boy was the team's daredevil, the fastest skier, the one who took the most risks, skied closest to trees and mountain fissures. He pursued Johann—first as a partner, to snap each other's boots into place, to follow each other down advanced trails. And then he made his move on Johann in a shared hotel room on the night before a race, fondling Johann beneath the blankets and masturbating him without speaking a word. They rarely spoke, according to Johann's account. They skied and touched each other silently, and Johann lived with the terror that his parents and brother would find out. When school ended, Johann moved to Berlin.

"What about your boyfriend?"

"I wasn't ready to be gay."

In Berlin, Johann threw off the constraints of his middle-class, churchgoing upbringing, transforming into a bisexual man about town, dating girls but experimenting with boys, drawn to reckless young men who preferred silent coupling with no follow-up. "It took me a while to figure out I liked

127

older guys, guys with class. Like you, Ronnie." At the same time, Johann became an entrepreneur in training. "I watched how people bought things and how they sold things." He observed peddlers in the streets, selling oranges and packages of cigarettes, the leather dealers, vendors of fake jewelry and stolen CDs. He took note of the drug dealers and whores, the subtle ways they advertised and negotiated. "I'm thinking all the time, this is what I will do. I will move things out of one country and into another. I can't work in a factory like my father…"

"I thought he was an engineer."

He added, without skipping a beat, "An engineer in a factory, designing all the things they make."

"What did they make?"

Johann turned his face away, as if ashamed to think of his father's occupation. I wondered what his father designed that could produce such a sheepish reaction. Lingerie? Atomic weapons?

Johann spoke: "Clocks."

He fast-forwarded to a crucial moment in his narrative, the epiphany that brought him to the United States, which coincided with the falling of the Berlin Wall. "I'm watching all these people climbing on the wall, beating it with hammers, with their fists, and I think, now you can do business anywhere, the world is one big market. And I'm stuck in the crowd. All I can see is this guy in front of me with a tattoo of a dollar sign on the back of his neck, and I think, this is—what do you call it?—an omen. It means dollars will be the money of the world and English will be the language, and I don't have any dollars and I don't speak English.'"

When his father died, Johann inherited some money. He kissed his mother goodbye, charged his brother with her care, and flew to New York, securing a job as a bellhop and working on his English.

"I tried to let myself be gay in New York," he reflected.

"But I had doubts. What kind of life do men have together, with no family? Nightclubs all the time? Smoking, drinking, taking drugs…"

"That's crazy," I interrupted. "Gay people don't hang out in clubs and take drugs all the time. Look at me."

Johann *looked* at me.

"What? It's not as if I use drugs twenty-four hours a day seven days a week."

Johann kept looking at me.

"I go to the gym. I have a *personal trainer*! Just because I get high every now and then doesn't make me some kind of…" I stopped speaking, unwilling to venture into the territory of what I was or was not. It seemed irrelevant, for on this night, with Johann lying in my bed, in my house, next to my grandmother's quilt, anything seemed possible, and what I had been was not nearly as significant as what I might become if only my life managed a slight turn, a gentle veering from the cliff's edge.

Johann left the bed for the bathroom, and I reflected on the similar elements of our histories. We believed we had made our own lives. As much as we loved our well-meaning families, we fled our respective small towns, bearing secrets and seeking adventure. We had our brushes with the rich and famous. We learned most people are ridiculous and self-centered, yet we prized our parents' values of kindness, good manners, honesty, and hard work. Each of us had one sibling, a brother from whom we were estranged.

When Johann returned he talked of his brother, painting a glamorous picture of a weekend race car driver who squandered his winnings on post-race parties. Johann—sending home money he had earned through prostitution—exhorted his brother to be financially responsible. He suspected that after their mother's death, his brother sold her jewelry, and then her furniture, to maintain his race car and buy presents for his sycophantic girlfriends. Johann stopped writing to his brother, and several months had passed without communication between them.

Only once, during this bedroom exchange of familial tales, did Johann let slip a hint of self-pity. He spoke of his most recent Christmas Eve. He had been to "the office" but hadn't managed to secure a date. Walking home along Sunset Boulevard to an apartment he shared in Hollywood, he encountered a young hustler, a naive Midwesterner who had been ejected from the bar because his blue jeans had holes at the knees, a violation of the dress code.

"Guess they never heard of Kurt Cobain," the young hustler joked to Johann, trying to pass off his poverty as a fashion statement. Johann felt sorry for the boy and invited him home. Johann's roommate was visiting family for the holidays, and the apartment, in a gritty neighborhood, felt lonely. It was, after all, Christmas Eve.

Johann let the boy shower and lent him a change of socks, as the kid's were filthy and damp. They started to have sex, but Johann was depressed, thinking about his dead parents, wondering if his brother would visit their graves and take flowers on his behalf. They fell asleep with the television playing. Johann awakened Christmas morning to a silent apartment, as the young hustler had stolen the television and Johann's watch, leaving his damp socks hanging over the back of a chair.

Johann did not dwell long in pathos. "I learn my lessons, Ronnie. I am an orphan, but I am strong. I am my own boss. If I want to go to the movies all day, it's okay. If I want to go to the beach to play soccer with some Mexicans, I go. I pay my bills, so I can do what I want. As long as I go to the office three or four times a week. If someone says to me, 'Come to Texas, stay at my dude ranch,' I can do it. If someone says, 'Come to Vegas, I'll buy all your chips,' I say, 'For sure.' Who gets to live like this? Going all over the world? Nobody. I do. And I have fun. Dallas, Vegas, wherever I go! I'll take you to Vegas, Ronnie.

Oh, we will have a good time! They have shows like you can't believe. They sink a pirate ship in a swimming pool, and these guys run around with lions and tigers all over the place. You tell me when, we go. Nothing stands in my way! I live a life of total freedom."

With this declaration, he flipped to one side and clasped his hands, as if praying, beneath his face. Within seconds he was breathing steadily, sleeping or pretending to sleep. I reached past his shoulder for the light, prepared to forgive him anything, even shutting me out so abruptly. He had, after all, revealed so much, putting aside the master's protective armor and speaking to me as a confidant.

Before I turned out the light, I noticed the retro-style alarm clock resting on my nightstand. I remembered how Johann had averted his eyes when I'd asked him about his father's factory and the objects he designed and how he'd said, finally, "Clocks." I realized he hadn't turned away with embarrassment, as I'd generously and romantically assumed. He'd been scouring the room for an answer to my question, like an actor stranded on the stage, forgetting his lines, searching for a prop.

Fifteen

Love comes in spurts. It hurts. It hurts.

—RICHARD HELL, *THE BLANK GENERATION*

I went to bed with Johann Number One: the German boy who worried about his irresponsible brother and agonized over the fate of his dead mother's knickknacks.

I woke up with Johann Number Two (or Twenty-two, or Forty-seven): the Los Angeles hustler who *hated* the sound of birds chirping in the morning.

"Why do they have to make so much noise?"

He showered in five minutes and packed his bag, wearing wraparound glasses with reflective lenses so he wouldn't—as he put it—"go blind from the crazy sun you got around here."

He said goodbye to my dogs. He liked them, although he critiqued their monogrammed collars, recommending something with spikes. He offered to send one of his own spiked collars to Sadie, his favorite, my rescued and surly Akita who occasionally killed cats. "We have a connection," he said.

We walked through Woodstock while gray-haired Rastas gathered on the Village Green and black-garbed artists lined up to buy lattes and tabouli wraps. No one looked askance at Johann in his Diesel jeans and black boots. Woodstockers were used to seeing rock and roller wannabes at the hardware store and post office.

I thought of the plans I'd nurtured a few days earlier to invite him to stay with me, even to move to the country, to

133

share my rustic life. I had felt hopeful after our Bastille Day dinner with Caroline and Armand, and during the hours of conversation, lying in my bed, surrounded by family artifacts, including my grandmother's hand-sewn quilt.

"Give me the city," Johann declared, as if reading my mind. "I can be what I want. I can *get* what I want." He planted himself on the sidewalk and stuck his hands into his pockets.

"When is the bus, Ronnie?"

"Twenty minutes."

He nodded, narrowing his eyes. My heart jumped when I thought he might ask to stay.

"Don't you have to go to the bank?"

"Uh…right." I had forgotten to pay him for visiting me, for allowing *me* to drive *him* around the countryside, to be hosted at parties, feted at meals, kept in my bed, held in my arms, kissed, sucked, rubbed, and loved. He had paused outside the largest bank in town, which happened to be my bank. When it came to money, he had the homing instincts of a cruise missile.

"Be right back," I said.

Inside the bank I cashed a check for two thousand dollars. I knew from haggling with owners of escort services that the price for an "overnight" fell between eight hundred and fifteen hundred dollars per night. Johann and I had been together four nights, two in the city and two at home, so two thousand dollars fell short of the going rate. But the sex between us had been occasional and halfhearted, especially when the drugs were finished. At home, we talked and slept. And wasn't he the one who had said—a long time ago, when he clarified the distinction between a prostitute and a gigolo—that he charged for sex, not friendship?

The bank teller smiled at me. "That's a lot of cash. Buying a car?"

"A motorcycle," I answered.

On the street, I slipped him the money. "When do I see you again, Ronnie?"

Our relationship had reverted to professional status. Perhaps it was the effect of the cash that had traveled from my hand to his pocket, or his undisguised eagerness to leave.

"The next time I come to L.A., I suppose," I answered coolly.

"If you want to have another vacation, you call me, right?"

I felt disinterest for Johann and disgust with myself, similar to the way I felt at the end of a drug binge, when the foil packets were empty and turned inside out.

"I'll call you, Johann."

I worked through Friday evening, then drove to my local gay disco intending to drink only two martinis. Standing at the bar, I thought about Johann vacationing on Fire Island with his sober and "classy" friend, my rival, Ethan. I pictured them dunking their feet into the surf, sitting in front of a beach bonfire, watching the sunset, which was a perfect sunset, of course, stripes of orange and magenta. I imagined Ethan older than myself, with a gray skunk stripe at the peak of his out-of-date pompadour, wearing an ascot at his neck and a signet ring on his hairy finger. I saw them in a "classy" bed-and-breakfast, waking up without hangovers, eating eggs Benedict or French pastry. Would Johann demand chocolate sauce for the pastry? Or was he reserved, relaxed, and noncombative when he was with Ethan? Were they happy? Did he complain about me to Ethan, the way he complained to me about Ethan's taste in music? *This guy. His name is Ronnie. All we do is take drugs all the time. He drives me crazy. Drugs, drugs, drugs! And you should see where he lives! He's got spiders in his bathroom! Ah, you see, Ethan, this is what I have to go through in my line of work. It's a good thing I'm compassionate.*

In the men's room of the disco I found Bucky, my drug dealer, who offered me a bargain price for an eight ball of cocaine; he wanted to unload so he could go home and crash. I paid three hundred dollars for three and a half grams of powder and asked if he had any Valium. My last bottle of

Clonopin was empty, rattling around the glove compartment of my car. Bucky didn't traffic in pills, but he offered a recipe for falling asleep after a binge.

"Drink half a bottle of Nyquil and take a long shower. Climb into bed wet. Your body has to expend energy to dry itself." Bucky's eyes were sunken, and dried saliva clung to the corners of his mouth.

"When was the last time *you* slept?" I asked.

"What day is it?" He sneezed and blood spurted out of his nose.

I embarked on a binge that lasted through the weekend. I snorted drugs and drank behind locked doors. I paced, watched porno, and delivered monologues to my anxious dogs. As dawn rose on Sunday, I headed for the bathroom, intending to scorch myself with a hot shower and go to bed wet, per Bucky's advice.

While I was in the shower, I heard the voices of my housekeeper and her daughter as they entered my kitchen. I thought of the cocaine spread on the butcher block, the rolled-up twenty-dollar bill, *Lumberjack Gang Bang* playing in the VCR upstairs.

I shouted, "Lizzy? I'm not here." *No, that's not right.* "I mean, I'm in here. The bathroom. I'm…" *What am I?* "Sick!" *That's for sure.* "I'm really sick and need to be alone today. Hello? Did you hear me?"

Silence. I wrapped a towel around my waist and peered out the bathroom door. No one was there. I snuck up to a window. The driveway was empty.

Hmm…

I had been mistaken. I snorted two fat lines to celebrate.

That's when I heard my stonemason—a strapping bodybuilder who often worked in nothing but gym shorts and work boots—outside, speaking in a low, conspiratorial voice. I thought I heard him say something about getting a ladder out of the barn, to look through the kitchen window.

I double-checked the driveway. No vehicle there except my own. I darted from window to window, scouring my yard for the brawny worker. The lawn was deserted, except for my lolling dogs.

Hmm...

I retreated to my bedroom with my bottle and my stash and locked the door. My bedroom was painfully bright with sunshine. Recently I had replaced all the windows; they remained uncovered, without shades or curtains. I removed bed linens from a trunk and nailed them where curtains ought to have hung. I crawled into bed, but the springs below my mattress crackled each time I moved. This wasn't so bothersome until I remembered that one of my overzealous workers had connected the springs of my bed to a sound system that blared each squeak through speakers mounted outside. I solved this problem by hunkering down on the floor of my bedroom closet, although I still heard the steps of booted feet walking on my roof. Each time I moved in the closet, even to shift my weight from one hip to another, the person walking across my roof stepped onto another roof shingle. Sometimes I heard a metallic click, which might have been any number of things, even the VCR shutting off in the next room, but sounded to me exactly like the cocking of a pistol. I figured out the game we were playing. If I moved, they moved. So I didn't move.

Dr. Yu's question from weeks ago floated about my mind: *Why you don't try to love man who is not a prostitute?* There were other questions, my own, which I translated into Dr. Yu's voice: *Why you drink so much? Why you take drugs? Who are those people on your roof?* I half expected answers to seep through the closet's cedar lining or tumble from the empty sleeves of jackets hanging above. But there were no answers in my bedroom closet, only recriminations. Only the facts. My life had taken on the material quality of the ads with which prostitutes promote themselves: all statistics and no explanations. I had emigrated to a world of forty-seven inch chests, nine percent body fat, and hairless bubble butts. No one asks why a butt should resemble a bubble; it just does. I wondered if I was losing my mind, if I would end up in a locked room with padded walls, and I realized that's exactly where I *had* ended up—the front door was bolted, the bedroom door was latched, the windows were covered, the closet was dark, and the hanging clothes provided padding.

I was home.

My great-grandfather had ended his days locked in the back bedroom of his daughter's house, deprived of alcohol too late to retrieve his sanity.

I coaxed this information from my grandmother during a phase in the 1970s when I became fascinated with my "heritage," encouraged by my feminist and Marxist professors from the University of Pittsburgh. Both my grandfathers had worked in the mines, and my father's father died of black lung. My grandfathers' histories held some interest, but they died before I learned I was supposed to revere them. Besides, they were *men*. In the politically charged era of the late 1970s, the only thing better than working-class history was working-class herstory. My father's mother was my only living grandparent, and she was a woman, and she liked to talk. I plagued her with a tape recorder for weeks.

Leota told me that her father had been the tenant farmer to a man known as the Captain. The Captain lived in a grand house, three stories made of brick facing the Ten Mile Creek, a tributary of the Monongahela River. I have seen a picture of my great-grandfather, one of those faded black-and-white photographs pasted to cardboard, in which he scowls in a turn-of-the-century way behind a bushy beard. In this image my great-grandfather and his wife do not look at each other, and one wonders, inspired by the queasy look on my great-grandmother's face, how many years passed in which they did *not* look at each other, inside and outside the photographer's studio.

Leota was born in the tenant farmer's house, a shingled cottage with a tar paper roof that faced the Captain's house from a respectful distance. When she married she moved into house that had been converted from a church, complete with a cemetery and Civil War graves. This house sat on a hill above the Ten Mile Creek, directly opposite the Captain's mansion and the tenant's cottage where she had been born. My grandmother liked to quilt and embroider and host prayer meetings, and she liked to talk about the past, although she lowered her voice when she spoke of her father.

"My mother had no choice but to leave him," she said, squinting through her good eye, stitching a patch for a quilt. "He chased us from the house with a shotgun. We left and I didn't see him for twenty years."

After two decades had passed, her father appeared on her doorstep, destitute and homeless. My grandmother took him in and locked him in the downstairs bedroom. She never told me about locking him up. I got this detail from my mother, who was thrilled to make this contribution to my grandmother's "herstory." My mother held a grudge against Leota for some long-ago slight, and she exacted revenge, finishing Leota's tale. "When I was dating your father, they wouldn't let me *near* that back bedroom. And believe me, they made sure that door was *locked*." My mother smiled, taking a drag on her cigarette. "They had to keep the girls away from *that* one."

My mother might have been accused of throwing rocks from inside a glass house. Her father was "senile," as we called it in those days. He paced his house, rattling the change in his pockets. He was obsessed with shoes, coveting the shoes of each man he encountered. My Uncle Bob, with the same shoe size as my grandfather's, inevitably left my grandfather's house in his stocking feet, with my grandfather proudly wearing Uncle Bob's shoes. Aunt Hazel, a spinster and caretaker for my grandparents, returned the shoes the next day.

My grandfather believed he lived in a nursing home. He called Aunt Hazel the "supervisor" and told visitors she never gave him enough to eat. My Aunt Hazel, who cared for aged parents, drunken brothers, abandoned nieces, and a dying sister-in-law, clenched her fists and declared through gritted teeth, "I just want to kill him when he says that." The most fabulous delusion I remember my grandfather describing was one in which three "colored" trapeze artists performed on a high wire in his bedroom.

My lecherous and imprisoned paternal great-grandfather and my change-rattling, delusional, maternal grandfather lived on opposite ends of one street. The walk between their houses took five minutes. My mother's brother, the drunk who drove his car into neighbors' houses, lived smack in the middle of the same street. His oldest daughter came down with a case of "nerves" at the age of three and was sent to live with my caretaking, forever put-upon Aunt Hazel and my nutty grandfather with his circus-themed hallucinations. Another of my aunts gave birth to an illegitimate daughter in the 1940s and was banished to Pittsburgh to become a "career gal." Her daughter was raised as my cousin and never knew, until she reached adulthood, the truth of her parentage. By the time her mother (whom she called her sister, even at her funeral) died, "senility" had been replaced in the vernacular by Alzheimer's, and it was striking down my mother's siblings without mercy, progressing ferociously and chronologically: each sister watched the one before her reduced to a drooling infant in diapers. As one of my aunts fed her sister pureed meat and vegetables from a white plastic spoon, she had already lost the ability to call the spoon a "spoon."

My closeted reverie was interrupted by the ringing of the telephone. I assumed it was another hallucination—probably a trick to draw me from my hiding place—until the answering machine picked up and I heard the voice of my producer on the Ashley Judd vehicle. He said our script was about to go into "turnaround," which is how they tell you in Hollywood that your work has been condemned and is being put to death.

I mulled the word *turnaround*. If I script can go there, I wondered, what about a life?

"Turnaround," I said, aloud. I elaborated, adding Dr. Yu's accent. "You go into turnaround? What you think? Possible? Huh?"

Then, I answered, in my own voice: "Shit, you asshole! You can't even stand up!"

It was true. My legs were locked in a pretzel shape, with my knees jammed against the closet's cedar lining.

Sixteen

I arrived at the Pittsburgh airport, nearly expecting my parents to meet me at the gate, as they used to do when I flew home for holidays or funerals. In those days they had cowered in a small-town attitude behind boisterous Pittsburghers, though I spotted them easily, thanks to my mother's sprayed-stiff nimbus of silver-white hair.

I had traveled to Pennsylvania after a call from a local hospital's emergency room. A nurse explained that my father had experienced a "cardiac episode." He had been wheeled away for tests, and according to the nurse, my mother seemed "a little out of it." My response was Pavlovian: I packed a bag and headed for the airport.

There was little in my life to keep me from my parents. My film projects were stalled, in turnaround, on hold, paused, or "simmering."

There had been an attempt to revive the Appalachian-themed script, but the meeting with a studio representative had not gone well. My director and I were presented with a mandate: What our script was missing, we were told with the authority of Yahweh delivering the Ten Commandments, was The Guy. Our main character, with the tintinnabulary name Rudell, struggles as a single mom after her husband deserted her. Her travails continue for forty pages or so until the husband shows up, barely apologetic, expecting to be welcomed back. Rudell's complicated reaction to his return constituted the drama of the third act. According to the studio, however, this structure was problematic. "It's a love story," the executive explained. "Where's the love?"

I might have been better equipped to receive this criticism if I had managed to sleep the night before, or even the night before that. But after all, *I* wasn't the one who had scheduled the meeting for nine A.M. on a Monday. In Nyack, New York. And despite assurances to the contrary, I was certain the air-conditioning system *had* malfunctioned, as there was no other explanation for the sweat that rolled from my hairline to my ears.

"Let me get this straight." I launched into my response. I saw my director shake her head—tiny little shakes of the head, meant only for me to see—indicating, I supposed, that I should stop speaking, but I did not stop speaking. "The script is about a woman who struggles to keep her family together when she becomes a single mom. It's just my opinion—and who am I, anyway? I'm just the writer—but don't you think that in order to make a movie about a single mom, doesn't that mean—God, I can't believe I'm sweating so much. Are you sure the air-conditioning is working?—doesn't the main character have to be, um, well, what's the word I'm looking for? *Single?*"

Soon after this meeting, the project was labeled "inactive."

"*Ron. Your father's in the hospital. Uh… Okay…*"
Click.

My mother had spoken into the answering machine as if someone had told her what to say and she was repeating it without comprehension, an entirely possible scenario. She grew more confused with each of my father's emergencies. A bout of angina or pneumonia (his) brought her to the brink of the most catastrophic event she could imagine—losing my father—and returned her, when it passed, with pieces missing, like a jigsaw puzzle you've lent to careless friends. My father survived his body's near-meltdowns, through intubation to extubation, from intensive care to rehab to home nurse visits. But with every crisis, my mother lost a bit of herself.

My father suffered congestive heart failure, arthritis, and chronic pulmonary disease; he endured knee replacements, disc removals, and the insertion of wire mesh into his stomach to stanch an ulcer. An operation on his intestines left him without a belly button. My mother and I spent more than one Christmas standing on either side of a hospital bed, unwrapping presents with my father, while I dangled ribbon from metal stands supporting I.V. bags.

My father had a Santa Claus belly, and his once-handsome Bavarian features had been distorted by flabby jowls, although his blue eyes remained youthful and curious. My mother was nervous, slender, and pretty; she wore tiny earrings and buttoned her blouses to the top. And, before Alzheimer's distracted her from regular grooming, she kept her white sneakers gleaming with daily applications of polish.

As a teenager, in our tiny house with vinyl siding and the shower in the basement, I had suffered the typical adolescent pangs of resentment toward my parents, felt them suffocating me with their small-town habits. I hated, for example, the way my father cut all the food on his plate at the beginning of a meal. I resented my mother when she insisted I wear a sweater on a 70-degree day in April because it was, after all, April. But later, when I left home to attend college, my loneliness and the distance helped me to appreciate my parents' manners as leftovers of a simpler era, and we became friends. They visited, bringing garden produce and casseroles, while I showed off Pittsburgh, which my father pronounced "Pixburgh," and introduced them to bagels, upscale burger joints, light beer, and Jews. For them—used to farms, coal mines, church socials, and Hunky weddings at the Volunteer Firemen's Hall—Pittsburgh might as well have been Constantinople (as a matter of fact, my father fell in love with falafel, which certainly did nothing good for his blocked arteries).

Attending graduate school at Columbia University, I hosted my parents in New York City. They settled on a bench near Lincoln Center, calling out front porch–style greetings—"Hello, there! Where are you running to?"—to Hare Krishnas, schizophrenics begging change, or members of cults wearing white swabs of turbans. My mother wagged her head and commented, "People in New York sure are different."

The changes at home were always for the worse, even when they were well-intentioned, such as the vinyl siding that covered the 130-year-old Disciples of Christ Church in the same shade of matte white that colored my parents' house, a lifeless tone that exists only in vinyl, hiding and precipitating the rotting of wood. The desolate center of town had been—decades earlier—an authentic town square, with a brick memorial honoring veterans of World War II that bore my father's name. But the memorial had been bulldozed, declared by the town council too difficult to maintain. Eventually, some local organization tried to spruce up the square by mounting a coal hauler onto a concrete pedestal and adding a bronze plaque that paid tribute to coal miners. The coal hauler must have become too difficult to maintain, like the veterans' memorial, as a tangle of poison ivy crept along the pedestal, while rust consumed the yellow-and-black machine. In a house facing the coal hauler lived one of my alcoholic uncles, still drinking and never eating solid food, thin as a Biafran, living on cans of a liquid dietary supplement. Though a recluse, he loved cats and kept several, although they inevitably died of feline leukemia, infecting each other, coughing up blood.

Long before the town had been devastated by "improvements," I wanted to flee. Although I cherished memories of my early childhood—when I was cute and skinny with good, straight teeth and too young to be considered effeminate, during that age when children are more or less unisex—my adolescence changed everything. There was no escape; the world was bordered by the Allegheny Mountains and the Monongahela River. Pittsburgh, 55 miles to the north, might as well have been located in another galaxy. And there were the afternoons at home with my brother when he tried to drive the "sissy" from me, bending limbs to the point of excruciation or squashing my face beneath a pillow.

I am living proof of the genetic predisposition toward homosexuality, as no discouragement—verbal or physical—was sufficient to alter my path. I preferred hiding in my room, drawing pictures of girls and imagining them in soft, pastel-colored angora sweaters and sparkling diamond necklaces to tossing and catching balls, thank you very much, and chose, one Christmas, for my all-time favorite present, a bicycle with three gears, butterfly handlebars, and an elongated, "banana" seat in sparkly purple. At least the bicycle was officially a boy's bike, with the required, potentially castrating bar. But it was colorful and glittery, like the jewelry worn by the girls in my drawings. No amount of pleading on the part of my parents in the toy department of Montgomery Ward could change my mind. I insisted on the purple banana seat with matching shimmering handle grips. My brother had the last word on the bicycle, however. On Christmas morning—while I dressed, preparing for my inaugural ride—he whisked the bicycle from under the Christmas tree to the street, coursing up and down the block on it, shifting the gears so roughly that they became stripped and useless. He dragged the mortally wounded bicycle back to the house as if lugging home the carcass of a some prey.

I found my parents in a room in the intensive care unit, in their usual positions: my father lying in a hospital bed, attached to I.V. lines and monitors, and my mother perched in a chair. My mother was accompanied by a neighbor, someone we paid (secretly) to tend to her when my father was away from home, which meant, exclusively, in the hospital. We were reluctant to leave my mother alone in the house, for fear she would burn it down. My Aunt June—the second of my mother's sisters to fall victim to Alzheimer's—was the main suspect in the fire that had consumed my grandparents' house on Christmas morning two years earlier.

My father's greeting caught me off-guard with its casual quality. "There he is. How was your trip?"

"Uh, okay."

My mother shuffled toward me with tiny steps, walking as I imagined Chinese women walked in the era of bound feet. Her smile seemed plastered to her face, inappropriate for the situation. "I'm so happy to see you," she said.

"I thought there was an emergency."

"I'm all right," my father shrugged.

"Then why are you here?" I wanted to say, "Why am *I* here?"

My father lifted his hands—I.V. lines and all—and dropped them back to the bed. "Who knows? I had some chest pains, but I'm fine. Did they feed you on the plane?"

At this point, the neighbor—a soft-spoken woman who tried to hide her obesity beneath pastel sweat suits—rolled her eyes at me, indicating something was amiss.

"I think I'll talk to a nurse."

My father was helpful. "My nurse's name is Glen. He's a nice guy. He farms. He's going to give me some homegrown seeds for lima beans. He's right out there, at the station." As I stepped out of the room, looking for Glen, my father called me back. "Hey, Ron," he said. "Before you go, look out the window." At this point the neighbor rolled her eyes a second time. I glanced out the window, to the parking lot.

"Yeah?"

With a straight face my father said, "Isn't that some ship?" I was confused. My mother was the one with Alzheimer's.

"Ship?"

"That ocean liner," my father continued. "They're having quite a party. I was thinking of swimming over there, but I don't think I'm invited."

The neighbor rolled her eyes a third time, and my mother kept smiling her dazed smile of incomprehension.

Glen the nurse was unimpressed with the report of my father's hallucination, dismissing it as the result of a temporary and benign syndrome known as intensive care unit psychosis. "All the monitors bleeping, bleeping. The lights. That stuff drives people crazy. Or maybe it's the steroids." My father's heart condition was a more serious matter; the organ was surrounded by fluid, and there might be blockages requiring balloons or stens. A cardiologist would elaborate in the morning.

"Your father says you garden."

"A little."

Glen took in my earrings and tattoos. "Bet you're into all that organic stuff."

I returned to my father's room, and he seemed perfectly lucid, asking me to escort my mother to the coffee shop for something to eat. He pulled me close, to whisper, and I expected another psychotic vision. Instead he warned me to hold my mother's hand and not to let her wander down any corridors by herself. "God knows where she'll end up."

I never completely credited my father's claims regarding my mother's decline. I knew she was sick, and I suspected one day in the not too distant future I would be scouting nursing homes, helping to make her worst nightmare come true. But I was willing to give her the benefit of the doubt, hoping to stave off the inevitable.

"Come on, Dad. She doesn't seem so bad."

"You don't know what I go through at home." Then he

murmured with lowered eyes, "And watch her in the coffee shop. She has accidents."

For comic relief, I said to my father as we left, "I guess, if you're not here when we get back, you'll be on the ocean liner."

"I told you I wasn't invited," he replied.

We said goodbye to the neighbor, and I led my mother to the coffee shop by the hand. She comported herself well. The symptoms of Alzheimer's, I was learning, were hit-or-miss.

The first sign of mental decline had appeared two years earlier when my parents visited me in Woodstock. They pulled up in their sedan and opened the trunk, as was the tradition, exposing a cooler filled with produce from my father's garden. Following my part, I looked for one of my mother's fruit pies, her specialty; she had been baking pies from scratch for forty years. But there was no pie in the cooler.

"Where's my pie?" I asked.

My mother replied, "I had to throw three pies away. I couldn't get them to come out right." With a laugh, she added, "I think I've lost my touch."

Two months later I visited my parents in Pennsylvania, and again, as was the custom, I asked for my pie. My mother's features turned hard and she spoke with finality: "I don't bake pies anymore." It was Alzheimer's first casualty.

But she seemed fine in the hospital coffee shop as she settled into the orange molded plastic booth. She ordered a hamburger and a Coke. "Boy, am I glad to see you." She had said it earlier, the exact words, but people often repeated themselves for emphasis. I wanted her to be fine. I hoped my father had been exaggerating her symptoms. He had a tendency toward overprotectiveness and was, after all, suffering from intensive care unit psychosis.

My mother clenched her drinking straw between two fingers and inquired, "Now, what is this?"

I was surprised by a violent surge of fury toward my parents as the realization hit home: I was saddled with two old, decrepit, loony people. My mind raced. Could I be compelled by the law to care for my mother and father? Was it possible to uncouple my life from theirs, rise from the booth, and walk out of the hospital, leaving behind the delusional man in the ICU and the addled woman in the coffee shop booth? Would my mother follow me? Or would she stay in the booth, waiting for my return, while the staff swept the floor and turned off the lights?

That image—my mother sitting in a sterile place, surrounded by strangers—diluted my despair; in fact, it melted my heart. It seemed a perfect metaphor for her experience: spending the rest of her life in unfamiliar places, waiting for someone to return, while the lights shut down one by one on the things she cared about or didn't care about, names of loved ones, everyday objects, baking pies.

I remembered the Christmas morning in which my brother had spoiled my bicycle. I couldn't control my reaction and started to bawl. My brother mocked me, imitating my weeping for the beloved bike, with dry heaves and exaggerated sobs. To my surprise, my mother intervened, saying that a boy in my position couldn't help but cry a little; I ought to be left alone. I was so startled by my mother's declaration that I stopped crying. No one had ever claimed *any* reaction of mine to be natural.

My brother turned on my mother, accusing her of turning me into a "baby," and instantly the argument was over. My mother dropped her eyes, muttering "Well..." My father, watching from the kitchen doorway, disappeared into the bathroom with yesterday's newspaper. My brother cast the wounded bicycle to the carpet, its spinning front wheel making the only sound in the room.

That night—Christmas night—my mother entered my room to hear my prayers. Usually she sat on the edge of the bed, and sometimes she held my hand. Remembering my brother's words and their effect on everybody—which, to me, confirmed their validity—I lay on my side, pretending to sleep. My mother said my name, but I didn't stir. She didn't try to wake me, and she never entered my room again to witness my prayers. Sometimes she stood in the doorway, a silhouette, and offered a "good night," but in time she gave up that ritual as well. We spoke "good night" to each other as I headed for bed with a library book, and she remained on the sofa, glancing through a magazine. She stopped fussing with my hair before church, no longer buttoned my jacket on a blustery day, and glanced away when my eyes met hers.

But, in the hospital coffee shop, watching her fumble with the wrapper of a straw, I was overcome by a sensation of love for my mother that was fierce, even sensual, and nearly primal; it surged through me, a need to protect her, a commitment to it, and a feeling that I could kill anyone who harmed her. This was, I supposed, how mothers were meant to feel toward children.

"It's a straw," I answered.

"And what do I do with it?"

I made a decision. It was a decision to *do* something as well as a decision *about* something. I decided that life was awfully short and the possibilities for pleasure were scarce. It wasn't, for example, important to analyze my tendencies toward excessive drinking and drugging. I was merely pursuing elusive feelings of exhilaration. I didn't have to try to capture Johann, to conform him to the structures of my life. It was important only to grasp diversion and gratification whenever possible. To be high and with Johann whenever possible. I resolved—when my parents' medical troubles had been downgraded below emergency level—to invite Johann to join me for another vacation, someplace urban and lively that didn't resemble the decomposing corpse of the town in which I'd been born.

I took the straw from my mother's hand. I could be gentle with her now and, later, patient with my father. They didn't own me. My heart had already taken flight to meet Johann in some mental version of Emerald City. I removed the straw's wrapper and dunked it into my mother's soda. "You put it in your drink. Like this."

My mother shrugged. "Oh." She drank from the straw, as if it was perfectly natural to put your lips around an object whose name and purpose you'd forgotten.

Seventeen

*Spanish traders en route to Los Angeles along the
Spanish Trail in the early 1700s sought a route that
would pass through the then unexplored Las Vegas
Valley. At the time, the Spaniards referred to the
route through the valley as 'jornada de muerte,'
journey of death.*

                        —CITY OF LAS VEGAS WEB SITE

LAS VEGAS, NEVADA—DECEMBER, 1996

I booked a room with a hot tub for me and Johann in the
Luxor Hotel, which sits at the end of the Strip in Las Vegas and
happens to be the largest pyramid in the Western Hemisphere,
outranking Chichen Itza, Uxmal, and Teotihuacan. Our room,
with a slanted wall, offered a view of the Sands Hotel, due to
be demolished by explosion at midnight on New Year's Eve. It
was not evident at a glance why the Sands Hotel faced the
wrecking ball, except—surrounded by pyramids, Greek tem-
ples, and Italianate palazzos—it stood guilty of resembling
nothing more than a hotel.

On the flight from New York, I sat next to a Peruvian woman
and her mother, who told me of their harrowing experience
with terrorists at home in Lima; the rebels had taken control of
the residence of the Japanese ambassador, which was adjacent
to their house, separated by a stone wall and a courtyard. The
daughter was petite and dark-skinned, conservatively but

                        155

expensively dressed, and educated, speaking near-perfect English. She held a plastic cup of apple juice in a manicured hand as she spoke, sitting erect, as if she could not relinquish the attitude of high alert she had assumed during her crisis. For ten days her family had been prisoners in their home, as the police forbade them to enter the street. They were notified by telephone to sleep under their beds, never to turn on a light, and to crawl on the floor beneath the windows. When machine-gun fire reported against the walls and once through a window, they squeezed beneath a bed, held each other, prayed the rosary, and cried. Finally the police negotiated their release, but it was terrifying, stepping into the street, into the clear view of the terrorists, who they feared might renege on their promises and open fire. The young woman shivered as she spoke of the escape, the despair she felt in leaving behind everything—clothes, toys, heirlooms, and photographs. She and her mother left the males of the family with relatives and went on a shopping spree to New York and Las Vegas, hoping to forget their troubles. She had been to Las Vegas many times and assured me—making my first visit—that I would love it, as it was a city where one could forget about bad times and ignore responsibility, and where there was little chance of running into terrorists. It was the kind of place where nothing important ever happened.

Months had passed since Johann had visited me in Woodstock. I had been occupied with the details of my parents' health care, consulting with cardiologists, pulmonologists, neurologists, respiratory therapists, physical therapists, occupational therapists, case managers, home health aid workers, visiting nurses, and what is known in Pennsylvania as an ombudsman, the person to call to complain about the treatment you're getting from everyone else.

My father's intensive care unit psychosis progressed beyond the mirage of an ocean liner to the conviction that he was imprisoned, with Glen the friendly nurse transformed into a hostile jailer. My father yanked the I.V. lines from his arms and dislodged the oxygen canula from his nose. Finally he had to be restrained and intubated; chemical sedation was applied sparingly, due to his respiratory problems. Seeing my father tied to his bed, with a tube deforming his mouth and another taped to his nose, reminded me of the days spent saying goodbye to my ex-mother-in-law, Gloria. His room was a replica of hers, with tubes entering comparable orifices, pumps and monitors emitting familiar, irksome sounds.

It was difficult to view my father in this situation, to press chips of ice against his lips and speak comfortingly, but nearly impossible to explain it to my mother; that is, to explain to someone who is losing her mind that someone else has lost his mind. The crisis cast my mother into periods of silence, focusing on her own needs, primarily to drink Coca-Cola and eat candy bars. At the hospital my mother stared at her knees and occasionally opened her purse, rummaging through it for nothing in particular. At home she retreated to the bedroom that used to be mine. She gazed at the television, which only intermittently she remembered to turn on. She kept a crinkled sack full of miniature candy bars and cashews stashed under the bed and gorged the contents, refusing other food. She made trips to the refrigerator where she maintained a glass of cola on a shelf, resting on a folded paper towel. She sipped the cola standing at the refrigerator with the door open and returned the glass to the shelf with a shaky hand, often spilling some but not seeming to notice. She refilled the glass from an open can of Coke, to the exact amount it had held moments before, then returned to her post in the bedroom to eat more miniature Milky Ways and Three Musketeers bars. Her conversation was reduced to a question and a request, which she repeated at ten-minute intervals and which seemed to bear for her the same significance: "Is your father going to be all right?" and "Can we go to the store? I need more Coca-Cola." Obviously, my father had been dealing with this behavior before his cardiac crisis, as I found several twelve-packs of Coca-Cola in the basement, stacked next to the furnace.

My father was detoxified from steroids, extubated, and discharged without elaborate intervention for his arterial problem, judged a bad risk for surgery. He was given pills to thin his blood, nitroglycerin tablets to dilate his arteries, and a nebulizer to clear his lungs. My parents' house took on the appearance of a makeshift hospital, the kitchen table laden with prescription bottles, the rooms crammed with portable oxygen tanks, a walker, supports for the toilet, a plastic chair for the shower, and forty feet of plastic tubing that led from an oxygen compressor to my father's nose. My mother's walking became less sure, her vision affected by Alzheimer's, and frequently she tripped over my father's oxygen line, yanking his head in one direction or the other. He yelped, "Jesus, Thelma, watch my tube!" My mother shouted in reply, "Oh, shit, Wayne, I didn't step on your damn tube!"

In order to care for my mother it became necessary to tell her lies. For example, we needed an official diagnosis of Alzheimer's from a neurologist in order to obtain the experimental drug Aricept, which was reputed to retard the disease's symptoms. My mother declined to see a new doctor, closing the subject with, "There's nothing wrong with me." I couldn't imagine dragging my mother into a doctor's office against her will. I mean, I couldn't imagine how to accomplish it. My mother was fit and strong. I plotted a ruse. I told her that every member of our family was seeing neurologists because Alzheimer's so obviously affected us, and that I, in fact, had an appointment with a doctor in New York. I added there was a new drug available for people who were in danger of coming down with Alzheimer's. I elaborated that this experimental drug prevented the illness from occurring altogether and that, quite possibly, all of us would be taking it soon. My mother stood at the refrigerator, glass of Coca-Cola in hand, calculating my words. She may have forgotten the point of a drinking straw, but she knew a lie when she heard one. She set her lips hard together, shaking her head slightly, mustering the courage to turn me down, but the proffer of hope melted her resolve: The drug might prevent her from turning into her drooling, pitied, incarcerated sisters. She relented with a shrug.

My parents' conditions progressed with a similar degree of inexorability but different rhythms. My mother's decline was steady, although muted by Aricept. She clung to bizarre behaviors—the hoarding, the gorging—and gradually introduced new ones, including an unprecedented fear of dark-skinned people, which led her to shout, while walking through a shopping mall, "Where did all these black people come from?" My father's health fluctuated. One day he was building a new plywood cover for his riding lawn mower and the next he was carted by ambulance to the hospital, when the prescribed number of nitroglycerin tablets failed to ease the throbbing in his chest. I commuted from Woodstock to southwestern Pennsylvania, a visiting master of ceremonies, organizing, haggling, and cleaning, the mundane, attendant activities of old age and illness.

A postcard from Johann brought me up to date. He had dropped out of school for a semester, and he had moved from a two-bedroom apartment in West Hollywood to an efficiency on La Brea that he shared with Peter, the Czech bodybuilder. This news surprised me, as it contradicted his life plan, in geographical terms, to move west, aiming for Beverly Hills. It seemed strange he would give up school when his self-image— the manner in which he distinguished himself from other hustlers—hinged on his persistent effort at self-improvement. I had no idea whether he actually attended USC business school as he claimed, but it was uncharacteristic of him to admit to any reversal of fortune. Dropping school and the easterly move were setbacks, but he expressed no dismay in the few sentences on the card which ended with this postscript: "I'm still available for a trip to Vegas." He signed off with, "Your pal," and next to his name drew a smiling face.

The card was waiting for me on my return from one of my trips to Pennsylvania, a particularly unsettling one in which my father and I had tried to convince my mother to wear adult diapers. I stood in my kitchen in the darkness of Woodstock winter, with ashened snow melting from my boots and the dogs begging to be fed, and decided to see Las Vegas with Johann, to submit to every urge I could conjure for hedonistic indulgence: to gamble, drink, drug, make love, and laugh at campy men in rhinestone-studded tights ordering lions and tigers to jump through hoops.

I made plans, consulted friends and a travel agent, booked a room and flights, gleaned information from a guidebook. I arranged with Johann our typical exchange. I purchased his ticket and paid for the hotel, while he bought the "stuff" (our code word for crystal that we used on the telephone). I imagined a vacation in which crystal meth played a part, but not the whole or even largest part. I had every intention of taking in the shows, shops, and restaurants, the theme park and the desert, forgetting that my intentions had failed me before.

I spoke to Johann the evening before we were to meet. I paged him, and nearly an hour passed before he called from the street; I heard traffic and police sirens. He sounded distant, exhausted, and slightly frantic, not unlike my mother's attitude of the last few months when she used the telephone. I wanted to confirm that he was set to meet me at the hotel, that he had the correct address and phone number.

"Yeah, sure, Ronnie. I got everything to make you happy. I'll see you in a couple of days."

"Tomorrow, Johann."

"Yeah, right, tomorrow. I'm a little tired. I've been busy,

Ronnie, really busy. I'm taking classes for acting. They make me really tired."

I laughed, thinking Johann had made a joke. He poked fun at the hustlers who imagined themselves actors, the body-builders who hoped to be the next Jean-Claude Van Damme.

"Are you laughing at me, Ronnie?"

"Aren't you making a joke?"

"What's so funny? You think I can't be an actor if I want? You think I don't have what it takes?"

I was silent. Then he changed gears: "Yeah, yeah, I'm joking. For sure. No, I'm not an actor..." He seemed to be trying to convince himself. "Okay, Ronnie. I have to go. I don't have much time on my phone card. I'll see you tomorrow. I'll bring everything you need."

He hung up before he heard me say something I only half meant: "Just bring yourself."

The Peruvian mother and daughter were on my mind as I taxied to the hotel and wandered through the lobby-cum-casino, searching for the correct bank of elevators, heading for my room in the largest pyramid in the Western Hemisphere. I couldn't imagine anyone traveling to Las Vegas for respite after a terrorist attack. It was evening, twenty-seven hours before the ringing in of the New Year, and the streets, the hotel's circular drive, the entrance, the check-in counter, and the casino joggled with life. There wasn't a space within view that wasn't crammed with signage, glittering with lights, no surface that wasn't metallic and coruscated, no sidewalk that didn't throng with pedestrians, no icon—from the Eiffel Tower to the Statue of Liberty—that hadn't been copied, miniaturized, and pressed into commercial purpose, no hand that seemed able to resist the siren call of a one-armed bandit, no dollar that could stay in a pocket, not one strip-show barker who wasn't barking. There was nothing about Las Vegas to inspire restraint, and I—coming from a cold winter in the Catskills, after a trying several months—could taste the crystal as I rode the elevator, imagining the erotic lift I'd feel after the first bump, and the smell of Johann's skin, the pliant quality I'd adopt with licking, nibbling, and sucking, and the complete release I might achieve from the awesome burden of being someone who didn't measure up, whose life wasn't turning out as planned, connected to humanity primarily through the care of two old, sick, dependent people.

Johann jumped out from behind the door as I entered the room, a game of hide-and-seek. "Ronnie, it's so good to see you!" The playful attitude seemed forced, and he dropped it quickly, getting down to business. "Okay, here's the plan. We call room service. We eat. Then, I'm sorry, but I have to take a nap." Off my look of disappointment he warned, "Don't give me a hard time or I'll tie you up and hang you from the ceiling."

"Thank God you're back to normal."

I lied. He appeared anything but normal. His skin was gray and his eyes were cradled by dark half-moons; he looked thin as he paced the room, jittery and ill at ease. "Okay, so maybe I've been partying for a couple of days. I need food, so what? I'll sleep, one, two hours, and then I'll be ready to play with you. I will not disappoint you."

He must have registered my unease, as I unpacked silently. "Oh, Ronnie, I almost forget. I got you a Christmas present."

He produced one of those glossy gift bags you find in card stores. I opened it and found a CD by a rock band named Prodigy and a cartoon book featuring the animated MTV stars Beavis and Butthead. The CD was inexplicable, perhaps a last-minute grab from an airport vendor. But the book made sense. Johann claimed that I reminded him of a minor character from the Beavis and Butthead series: a bespectacled, guitar-playing hippie schoolteacher, a soft-headed quoter of Thoreau, the constant brunt of practical jokes.

"When that guy comes on, I always say, 'There's Ronnie!'"
The gift was classic Johann, a rose with a thorn. But it was a gift nonetheless.

"I don't have anything for you."

Johann revealed a desperate few seconds of disappointment; he dropped his eyes and his shoulders slumped forward. Clearly he had expected a Christmas present, and I stood before him empty-handed. As far as I was concerned, Christmas had passed in Pennsylvania, with my parents and relatives, surrounded by stacks of adult diapers and medical apparatus. My vacation with Johann was an antidote to Christmas. I remembered Johann's description of his own bleak Christmases, robbed by another hustler, passing hours in a movie theater alone. He had related the stories as examples of his independence and fortitude. But I questioned those claims. It was clear from the look on his face that he had hoped for his own glossy gift bag with a CD or a book, something beyond the meals, the airplane ticket, and the price of a hotel room; in other words, something more than the typical offerings from a client to a prostitute.

Each of us was embarrassed. We were always at odds, riding different rhythms; I'd acquired another relationship that had become burdensome. I stared at the king-size bed and yearned to sleep for at least a week.

Johann offered another solution. "Here's your real Christmas present." He dug into his suitcase and retrieved a sock, tied in a knot.

From the sock he produced several small, transparent plastic bags holding powder in colors that ranged from pale pink to yellow to dirty white. He dropped the bags onto the bed's starched sheet, assigning each a name and a dominant characteristic. The pale pink powder was called "champagne" and "makes you horny." The yellowish powder was "glass" and "mellows you out." The dirty-white powder, "chalk," promised to "keep you going for days." Johann reached into his suitcase for accessories, reminding me of a salesman who used to visit my parents' home, peddling kitchen rugs and bath towels from the trunk of his car. He retrieved a bottle of saline solution to keep our nostrils from being dried out by the crystal; a container of Vicks VapoRub for our noses and upper lips, to prevent them being burned as we snorted; and bottles of water to fight dehydration. Johann made his presentation with pride. "I know how to do crystal, Ronnie." The truth of his claim was evident. He had become a student of tweaking, a connoisseur of crystal. He had become *crystallized*.

I suppose there are some people who—locked in a hotel room with a prostitute and several grams of an euphoria-inducing compound—might have the fortitude to say, "What about our plans to see Siegfried and Roy?" But I'm not one of them. Siegfried and Roy were forgotten, along with the rooftop roller coaster, a sinking pirate ship, Wayne Newton, and Cirque du Soleil. During the twenty-four hours that followed the opening of the first bag of crank, my world was restricted to the dimensions of the hotel room's king-size bed. There was an occasional foray to the bathroom, which lay several feet away or, mysteriously and alternatively, in another dimension, with its too-bright lights and cold tile floor producing an unwanted connection to the obtrusive material world.

I lay on the bed, sometimes floating two inches above it. My eyes were open, seeing through the walls of the room to outer space, a blackened expanse with occasional stars that resembled sprinklers and smoke detectors. Or, my eyes remained closed, although I managed during these periods to peer *through* my eyelids, which had become transparent. Johann kept his distance, occasionally entering my awareness as a satellite, trapped in his own orbit, gawking at the television, staring out the window (When did the room acquire a window? When did it become a room?) or lying next to me on the bed, within arm's reach and unbearably close, so close I felt as if I might suffocate.

Once, when Johann lifted a pillow, I thought he was about to place it over my face to murder me, and I clamped my eyes shut in terror but was defeated by my transparent eyelids, condemned to witness my own execution. But Johann punched the pillow and replaced it beneath his head to prop himself up in order to watch a televised promo for Las Vegas sights.

There was no possibility that Johann and I might make love. This batch of crystal was too hallucinogenic and aggressive. I wasn't sure what I was made of and spent hours pondering the possibilities. Was I a mass of thoughts and impulses wrapped in skin? But the idea of skin seemed ridiculous. What *is* skin anyway? A kind of packaging, obviously, but where does it open and close, how does it fit so precisely? Does it involve a hidden zipper? Is it like a pressurized space suit, in which one puncture will cause the contents to disgorge, with a hiss, into the vacuum of space? This thought paralyzed me: that I was contained in something as fragile as skin, which I knew could be penetrated by a razor, scissors, a splinter, even a fingernail. I lay still, determined not to touch my own skin but wracked by the realization that my skin was touching itself, in my armpits, my scrotum, my jowls, and around my toes. My skin was its own worst enemy. The idea of touching another person's skin was unthinkable. When I considered it, I imagined two overinflated balloons rubbing together and heard the squeaking of their translucent surfaces, the popping and hissing as the contents, the trapped air, escaped. This is what I thought would happen if Johann touched me: I might pop like a balloon, and the contents of myself, that is, my thoughts, impulses, ideas, and memories— along with a fair amount of blood and tissue—would splatter over the room and at the same time into outer space, which was somehow the same thing.

On the afternoon of the 31st—New Year's Eve—I reentered Earth's atmosphere. I stood naked at the toilet, my toes curling against the tile floor, trying to pee. This respite of consciousness came without warning. For the most part, I was relieved to be alert, no longer consumed with pondering circular, inexplicable realities, such as the penetrability of my own skin. There was, however, a small problem. I was having a heart attack.

I staggered to the main room. Johann was staring at the television. "Don't freak out," I said. "But I've got these pains in my chest. It's hard to breathe. I think I'm having a heart attack."

Luckily, Johann was orbiting my own galaxy and responded quickly, not revealing the smallest hint of alarm (which alarmed me). He stood, stretched, and—with a yawn—said, "I know what to do."

He guided me to the bed. I felt his fingers on my arm and realized I missed his touch, that the crystal-induced paranoia had separated us. I wondered what Johann was planning—so calmly—to do. CPR? Call 911?

He opened a container of Vicks VapoRub and spread it over my chest with three of his fingers. He rubbed softly, in circles. "I don't think you are having a heart attack. But sometimes crystal makes you feel this way. Too much, Ronnie. You disappeared. I waited for you to come back, but when you did, even for a minute, you went to the stash. Another bump, another bump. Why didn't you want to play with me?"

He had been right about dehydration. Every ounce of water had been drained from me. I couldn't speak, as I couldn't pry my tongue from the roof of my mouth. And I certainly could not cry. I managed to whimper "I'm sorry."

Johann continued, "Now you will sleep, an hour or two. You are breathing better now?"

Another whimper. "Yeah."

"When you wake up, we'll start over. We'll snort a little crystal, just enough to let us have fun. Okay? We'll take it easy. Now, Ronnie, close your eyes. Close your eyes and rest."

I was happy to close my eyes as Johann instructed, to feel his fingers on my chest, and to drift in the medicinal, pungent aroma of Vicks VapoRub. I believed in Johann's healing powers, his desire for me, and his promise to wait for me to recover so that we could "have fun," snorting just the right amount of crystal, just the right amount.

My eyelids had recovered their opacity, and I drifted toward an overdosed, exhausted form of sleep. But, like Lot's wife, I couldn't resist watching Johann when he stopped rubbing my chest and—thinking I was asleep—walked to the stash, cut two large bumps and snorted them forcefully, tossing his head back to savor the effect.

Eighteen

The real trouble started on the street at an hour after midnight. The sidewalks were jammed. No one seemed to have a destination, in the anticlimax of the big twelve o'clock moment, when the Sands Hotel had detonated and spectators cheered, raising their fists in gestures of victory, as if the defunct establishment had been the loser in some sports event. People meandered along the Strip, aimless and grumpy, desperate to find something else to cheer. But nothing promised to explode, and there was a feeling of restlessness among the crowd; husbands snapped at wives and strangers shoved each other in the crosswalks, withholding apologies.

Johann was a leather jacket just ahead of me, hands jammed into pockets, forging through strangers with his shoulders. Because we had entered the Strip near our hotel, at the bottom of a rise, I could look past the permed and gelled heads and baseball caps to glimpse more of the same crabby, sluggish group that contained me and Johann, like standing on Earth, *in* the Milky Way, and looking to the sky and *seeing* the Milky Way.

Johann tugged my sleeve. "Careful, Ronnie. That guy has a camera."

I followed Johann's glance toward an overweight sightseer in a San Diego Padres sweatshirt, with a video camera slung over his shoulder.

"So?"

Johann regarded me as if I was an idiot. "He has a *camera*." He ducked his head, speaking low. "Let's take a taxi."

"Where?"

"Back to the hotel."

The Luxor was within view. "The hotel is right over there, Johann."

"*Where?*"

I pointed. "There." I wanted to ask how he couldn't manage to see the largest pyramid in the Western Hemisphere but thought better of it.

"All I'm asking is we take a taxi."

Johann rarely asked for anything. He made demands and gave orders. I explained that we might have to wait hours for a cab, while we could walk to the hotel in a matter of minutes. I spoke firmly, trying not to sound angry, adopting the tone I had developed while dealing with my parents ("No, Dad, you're not in a prison, you're in a hospital and all these people are trying to help you, but we can't help you if you keep pulling out the tubes."). I managed to steer Johann back to the hotel, through the crowded casino, into an elevator, and to our room.

But the room was no refuge for Johann, who paced, sitting here and there, on the bed, the sofa, the chair, scrutinizing the ordinary features of a hotel room—fire sprinklers, smoke detectors, light switches, doorknobs, the television screen—as if each object held a malevolent purpose. When Johann spoke, it was in a whisper. "Ronnie. Don't stand in front of the television. They can see you." He nearly jumped out of his skin when the unsupervised children next door began roughhousing and squealing. A locked metal door connected our room to theirs, and Johann pressed himself against it. He warned me that someone was listening through the door. I said, "*You're* listening through the door." A drunk in the street raised a hoarse and slurred refrain of "Auld Lang Syne," bellowing the last line as if daring someone to order him to be quiet, which no one did. The rising cacophony—genuine noises, heightened in their noxious qualities by the crystal, but certainly not hallucinations—twisted Johann's paranoia tighter. He paced. He turned the television on and off. He stood by the door. He peered out the spy hole. He asked me questions, not meeting my eyes with his, as if he was embarrassed. "Ronnie? Is that a camera?" he inquired, pointing to a smoke detector. For some reason (my long nap, the walk outside the hotel) I was nowhere near Johann's level of unreality. I was pleasantly buzzed and slightly aroused; in other words, I had achieved the high crystal is meant to deliver. I was alert and conscious. I was happy and ready to party. I was tweaking.

A social worker had encouraged me to be forthright with my mother when confronting her delusions. "No, Mom, there are no holes in the floor. But *you* see holes in the floor because you have Alzheimer's disease." Or, "Yes, Mom, you do know how to use a toilet, but you've *forgotten* because you have Alzheimer's disease." This technique had failed with my mother, as her protests—against walking across a particular floor at a particular moment or having anything to do with that porcelain object in the bathroom—were delivered with screams, cries, clawing, pleading, and cursing. There was little time for explanations offered in a social worker's version of a soothing (and, in my opinion, patronizing) tone of voice.

But part of Johann still belonged to the master, so his delusional observations alternated with periods of enforced calm as he stood rigidly, clenching his fists, trying to control himself, or perched nervously on the edge of a chair, facing the television, racing through channels with the remote. In these quiet moments, while Johann struggled for self-control, I offered social worker–style admonitions.

"These weird thoughts you're having," I said, "it's the drugs. The fire sprinkler is just a fire sprinkler, but you *think* it's a camera because the drugs are *making* you think it's a camera."

"Right, Ronnie. I know you are right." He nodded his head vigorously, at about the same rhythm with which he flicked his thumb against the remote, sending the television into a weird kaleidoscope of images. In the corridor the temporarily orphaned children had taken one of the elevators hostage, obstructing the doors and causing the elevator's bell to *ding* repeatedly. This *dinging* nearly matched Johann's rhythm with the remote and seemed for a moment to be connected.

Johann pointed to a smoke detector. "But that really is a camera, right?"

"No! It's not!"

Johann threw the remote at my head. It missed.

He reached for the telephone.

"Who are you calling?"

"Ethan." He referred to his friend/client in New York, the conservative designer who listened to classical music and did not use drugs.

I pressed the receiver's button, cutting the line. "It's four A.M. in New York."

Johann's body curled as if he was in physical pain. "Ethan doesn't care when I call. I can call him *any* time!"

Johann and I faced each other, connected by a few feet of telephone cord. He held the telephone's handset, while I kept my finger on the body of the machine, killing the line. It was a standoff, only Johann's hands were trembling and his eyes were rimmed with tears. I was used to following his commands and trusting his intuition during sex or while chasing drugs in dangerous sections of various cities. But his intuition was failing; his grip on reality had become detached, while mine felt surer.

"Please, Ronnie," he whimpered.

I didn't want him to call Ethan, to awaken Ethan on New Year's Day to announce that we were high on drugs in Las Vegas and things had gotten out of control. I often entertained visions of Johann and Ethan nesting on a sofa, listening to Mozart or watching rented movies, in their right states of mind, free of chemical influence. It was the kind of life with Johann that filled my fantasies. Our drugged adventures were meant to be stops along the way, a sowing of wild oats, until

we settled into a domestic routine, the kind of routine that—
in my imagination, at least—Johann shared with Ethan.

I took the telephone from his hand. "I don't think that's a
good idea." He dropped his hands to his thighs and mumbled
something incoherent. I made a suggestion: "Maybe you'd feel
better if you washed up."

He plodded toward the bathroom, pliant, deflated.

He washed, brushed his teeth, and applied gel to his hair.
He seemed no longer plagued by hallucinations; if he was, he
kept them to himself. I saw him glance at the air-conditioning
unit with suspicion, but he swallowed any paranoid commen-
tary. Once I caught him glancing at me with the same quizzi-
cal look. Did he imagine cameras behind my eyes?

"Ronnie. I'm going for a walk." He dropped the volume of
his voice and asked, "Do you want to come with me?"

Johann needed me, and he expressed it plainly. It ought to
have been a moment of triumph. He waited for my answer,
deciding between two jackets, his black leather, which he had
been wearing the night we met, and a denim jacket with a record
label logo, the gift of another client, a music industry executive.
Oddly, Johann's leather jacket no longer seemed to fit. When he
put it on, his shoulders disappeared; he looked like a child trying
on his father's clothes. He opted for the denim, although it made
him look ordinary, unadorned. With his slicked hair; pale skin;
darting, nervous eyes; and the slumped posture he adopted with
his paranoia, he resembled a refugee from Central Europe,
someone with an expired visa.

I yearned for the peace I would find in the room when he
was gone, the high I might achieve with a few more bumps of
crystal; there was plenty of colored powder left in the bags on
the nightstand, next to a straw we had taken from the room
service tray. I imagined how I might retreat to an obliterated,
crystallized state of mind, where I was parentless, siblingless,
friendless, loverless, and Johannless, to the indulgent, respon-
sibility-free zone that was the promise of Las Vegas, according

to the brochures, travel agents, television promos, and my fellow passenger on the flight from New York, the Peruvian woman seeking refuge from terrorists.

"I don't want to go for a walk."

He buttoned his denim jacket nearly to his neck and then reversed the procedure, finally settling on a particular look, two buttons near the bottom closing.

"I'll get a sandwich. A couple of sodas." He put his arms around me. "I'll be back in twenty minutes."

I opened the door for him. He paused, seeing the children who belonged to the room next door hopping in and out of the elevators. The doors to an elevator closed on them, catching them by surprise, and they disappeared, giggling. With the coast clear, Johann made his way down the corridor. He stepped softly on the carpet. He never glanced back. He looked, from behind, like an old man. When the elevator arrived he stepped into it.

I never saw him alive again.

Earth

Nineteen

I couldn't sleep in my bed. I couldn't accept the warmth of the duvet, with heat-trapping Dacron particles (an improvement on goose down, according to the catalog), nor the softness of its flannel cover. I couldn't bear to rest my head against my Ralph Lauren pillows in their 350-count Egyptian cotton cases. I despised my bed with its matte black iron headboard and firm mattress that was guaranteed to last my lifetime if I turned it every eighteen months. There was no comfort in my bedroom with its mission-style bookcase and wide-plank floorboards, with framed family photos and mementos on the walls and windows sealed against frigid air. A register directed warmth from a forced-air furnace (also warranted in writing) to my bedroom through an antique register cover, which had been treated with acid and scraped with steel wool to remove paint but not repainted, a touch of premeditated rusticity.

I haunted my house, a mournful specter, returned from Las Vegas two days early with a funeral to arrange. I didn't rattle chains but carried a bottle of tawny port wine. I decided I could not sleep in my comfortable bed, in my warm bedroom, while Johann lay (as I imagined him) on a cold steel table in a mortuary. The mortuary wasn't imagined. It was called the Palms, and a man named Kevin who worked there was waiting to hear from me regarding plans for Johann's remains.

My living room is the coldest room of my house, with a bay window that leaks and sliding patio doors that need to be replaced. I lay on the bare floor in front of the patio doors. I

177

made no use of a pillow, resting my head on the unforgiving wood and covering myself with a sheet (not a white sheet, as I imagined the sheet covering Johann, but pale blue, worn through and faded, headed for the rag bin). The frayed sheet covered me imperfectly, allowing cold air to tease my ankles. I imagined tying a tag around my big toe, something I had seen in the movies. I imagined writing "Dead Person" on the tag. I drank port wine and hovered between the comforting mental numbness provided by the wine and the bracing cold of the floor. I decided I was too comfortable. I opened the sliding patio door two inches and lay exposed to winter, feeling triumphant when my teeth began to chatter.

After Johann had left the room in Las Vegas, I managed a crystal-hazed imitation of sleep, sinking into bed and drifting in darkness. Within an hour, I was awakened by the telephone and a man's voice—a deep, in-charge kind of voice—identifying himself as "a detective."

"We need to speak to you. We're coming up to your room."

I was naked. There were several bags half-filled with crystal meth lying around somewhere. "I'm not dressed," I protested. "Is something wrong?"

"Please get dressed. We'll come up in five minutes."

There was no room for argument. I showered, dressed, and hid the stash in my suitcase (it didn't occur to me to throw the drugs away). The situation seemed serious. Perhaps Johann had gotten into a fight; maybe his immigration status was involved. I checked the hidden drugs three or four times, making sure they were secured away and no residue was left on a table or nightstand. I swallowed bottled water so my throat wouldn't feel so dry and slathered my chapped lips with cream. I breathed deeply to keep my hands from shaking and prayed I would not perspire.

A man entered my room and identified himself as Howard Frankel, an officer with the Las Vegas coroner's department ("coroner" is not a word one wishes to hear at four in the

morning on New Year's Day). Behind Mr. Frankel stood two
hotel managers, a man and a woman, in male and female ver-
sions of the same brown suit. Mr. Frankel wore pressed chinos
and a crisp windbreaker; nothing about him was tentative. As
he shook my hand, I wondered if my pupils were dilated, an
aftereffect of crystal, or whether there was powder residue on
my nostrils. There were introductions; the brown-suited hotel
managers had names that I instantly forgot. The female manager's eyes rested on the king-size bed and she nodded with
some kind of understanding, as if calculating the meaning of
a single bed in a room registered to two men.

"I'd like you to sit down." Mr. Frankel's voice had a professional, calm quality, like an announcer for public radio.

"What's wrong? Where's Johann?"

"I can't tell you anything until you sit down."

I began to sweat at my hairline, my upper lip, and under my
arms. No good news can follow such a command. The hotel
managers stood before the closed door, ready to make their
escape or block mine. Mr. Frankel placed a hand on my shoulder and guided me toward a chair. There seemed no way to fend
off the gesture, and I wondered if he had learned it during his
detective training in a seminar called "Breaking Bad News."

Mr. Frankel sat on the edge of my bed—the bed I had
shared with Johann, barely touching, except for the few
moments in which he had applied Vicks VapoRub to my
chest—and told me the facts as he knew them. Johann had
died on the Las Vegas freeway. He had stepped in front of a
pickup truck. The man driving the truck—who had an unfor-
gettable first name, Otis—had been traveling within the speed
limit, about sixty miles an hour. Johann's neck was broken. He
had been carrying the key to our hotel room, which allowed
them to find me. These facts were reported by Mr. Frankel
over my weeping. He paused now and then, when my sobs
took on a heaving quality. My cries drove the hotel managers
to the anteroom off the bedroom, where Johann and I had

stacked our luggage and where the glycine bags of crystal were hidden in a zippered side pocket of my suitcase.

Mr. Frankel asked questions and recorded my answers in a notebook. How were Johann and I related? I gave staccato answers, slurred out of thick lips and a stinking, dry mouth. "Friends," I said. Had we been drinking heavily? No. Was he taking drugs? Not that I know of, I answered, deciding truth was irrelevant at this point.

The next question took me by surprise, if it is possible to experience surprise when one is in a state of shock. "Did you and your friend have an argument this evening?" I noticed the television remote, on the rust-colored carpet, where it had lain since Johann threw it at my head.

"No. Why?"

Mr. Frankel shifted closer, intending, I supposed, to offer comfort.

"Let me try to explain this. I've got to write a report. I've got to classify this fatality. It seems like an accident. But there are questions…"

I stared at my socks. I couldn't let Mr. Frankel see my eyes for fear of what they might give away.

"The fact that your friend ended up on the freeway, well, it's difficult to understand. When he left this hotel, he could have gone to his left, up the Strip. But he turned to his right. There's nothing to the right but desert. So your friend walks into the desert. In the dark, at three in the morning. Where is he going? Why cross the freeway? Why choose this moment, when a truck is coming? I'm wondering if you and your friend had an argument. Was he in some sort of trouble? Depressed? I'm struggling to piece it together so I can close my report."

I didn't speak. In fact, I retreated from that room, from my own body, ignoring Mr. Frankel with his social worker's, compassion-for-hire style, ignoring the hotel managers with their disapproving looks and cheap brown suits. I relied on the residue of crystal and my memory of the recent trip I'd taken, while tweaking, into outer space; I remembered how the room had opened up and crystal had propelled me into the atmosphere. I remembered I had the ability to leave my body while appearing to remain in my body, and I realized I'd acquired this talent long ago, before I smoked crack or snorted crystal methamphetamine. I thought of my brother placing a sofa pillow over my face and how the hard wooden button at the center of the pillow had flattened my nose and how the ribbed fabric had filled my mouth. I remembered how I'd departed my body during those events—my "pain training"—floating toward the ceiling of my childhood home or escaping the room altogether, lighting on the branches of the maple tree in our front yard. Mr. Frankel and his inquiries and the hotel managers with their disdain fell away, along with the room's furniture, the oversize television, Johann's leather jacket slung over the back of a chair. I remembered Johann gelling his hair, pulling the cuffs of his jeans over his boots. I remembered his voice humming "Happy Birthday." I thought of the way he walked on the night we met, resembling a prizefighter entering the ring. I knew too that his swagger was camouflage. I had heard Johann's private laments: the lonely Christmases, the orphan boy's yearning for the dead mother who had adopted him. I had seen him tortured by crystal-induced, paranoid hallucinations. I knew that Mr. Frankel's suspicions about Johann's death were based in fact; that Johann might have wanted to die. I knew as well that he might have been confused, running from imagined demons, hearing voices or even footsteps behind him, as he had heard voices and felt watched in our room. I knew any theory of Johann's death might be true and that there was no way to choose one over the other and there never would be. And most of all I knew I was privileged to hold Johann's secrets and that I must not relinquish them, not yet, not to the corporate indifference of the hotel managers and not to Mr. Frankel's practiced compassion.

I returned to my body, to the hotel room, to the interview with Mr. Frankel. I adopted a posture I imagined Johann might have chosen in a similar situation. I straightened my spine and spread my shoulders. I was still crying; the tears poured forth, silently, one element I could not master. I spoke through a clogged throat. "There's no reason I can think of that my friend might want to kill himself."

Mr. Frankel asked about Johann's family. I told him about a brother in Europe, in Germany, I believed. I had no address for him. He told me they would have to contact the brother, as any decisions regarding Johann's remains had to be made by a relative. He gave me some business cards, including information about the mortuary where Johann had been taken. He offered the services of a grief counselor from the coroner's office, which I turned down. Then he asked me to point out Johann's possessions.

"Why?"

"They have to be returned to his family."

"I'll take care of them."

Mr. Frankel was firm. "You're not family."

I felt sick and weak, no longer able to resist the authority of a confident investigator from the coroner's office, wearing clean, pressed chinos at four in the morning on New Year's Day. I pointed out Johann's suitcase, socks, some briefs in a drawer, and shirts hanging in the closet. I became scrupulous in identifying each of Johann's belongings, his toothbrush, his Calvin Klein cologne and a ball cap with the letter J above the bill. The hotel managers left without speaking a word to me. Mr. Frankel shook my hand and regarded me, I felt, with genuine sympathy, inviting me to call him with questions. He left the room with Johann's suitcase, full of everything Johann brought with him except for my Christmas presents—the CD and the Beavis and Butthead book—and the bags of crystal hidden in my suitcase. There was no evidence that Johann had occupied the room except for a glossy stain of hair gel on his pillow.

I left Las Vegas within two hours on a flight arranged by my travel agent in New York, whom I roused from bed—as her husband pointed out, when he answered the phone—"at six. a.m. on New Year's Day." She offered to fly to Vegas to retrieve me, but I declined, wanting to leave as quickly as possible. I checked out of the hotel through an express service on the television and took a cab across a freeway to the airport, realizing later that it was the freeway on which Johann had died.

Before leaving the room I flushed the crystal down the toilet, although there was a moment of hesitation, with the half-filled bags in my hand. The crystal offered respite from the dreadful, contradictory chant that filled my brain: "Johann is dead. Johann can't be dead." My ability to escape my skin and these punishing thoughts had vanished; I couldn't get the words from my mind. Nor could I halt the alternating rhythms of hope and fear; one minute convinced that I was the victim of a joke or a particularly extended hallucination, and the next overwhelmed with the obvious reality of Johann's death. I embroidered the fact of his death with more, consequent facts: that never again would I touch his inner thighs, kiss his chest, smell the back of his neck. I was struck by two simple regrets: Never had I said to him, "I love you," and never had I kissed him on the lips. I cringed at the memory of the hours that had passed in the hotel room when I avoided his touch altogether. I concluded that the pale-colored powder in the tiny plastic bags was responsible for this last injustice, and I dropped the bags into the toilet and flushed.

It didn't occur to me to visit the mortuary, to view Johann's remains, until I was in the air, huddling at a window, garnering looks from other passengers as I wept. Whatever coolness had prevailed during my interview with Mr. Frankel (which might have been less cool than I remembered) had faded; perhaps the crystal in my system had been holding me together. On the plane I fell apart. I dug my fingernails into my palms to keep from screaming. I couldn't imagine how I'd left Johann behind.

At home, my medicine chest contained the tools of oblivion, Vicodin and prescription-strength Benadryl, which I had stolen from my father's trove of pills during a recent visit to Pennsylvania. I washed them down with port wine. The combination was stultifying; I moved slowly, and everything sounded muffled, including my own thoughts. In moments of encroaching sobriety, I replayed the last hours of Johann's life, revising my actions, searching for the deed or words that might have changed the evening's outcome. If I had joined him for a walk as he had asked... If I had taken his hand, led him to the bed and held him... Daylight hours were bearable; I feared nothing during the day but my mental recriminations. At night, however, the borders shifted and my accusers became supernatural as well as psychological. I believed that Johann stood in my backyard beneath an old pear tree that bore inedible, shriveled fruit, an escapee from purgatory, watching the house, scowling, demanding justice or, at least, my company.

Oblivion was postponed by a telephone call from Kevin, a dulcet-voiced mortician from Las Vegas. Had Johann's family made any decisions regarding a funeral?

I spoke impulsively and somewhat off the point: "I want to bury him next to his mother."

"That's beautiful, Ron."

"He loved his mother. He missed her. When she died, he couldn't afford to fly home for the funeral. I want to take him home."

"Ron, that's so generous. You're a good friend. By the way, where *is* Johann's home?"

"Somewhere in Europe. Germany. I think the southern part." I felt Kevin nodding on the other end of the line. I felt his patience. "I have to find Johann's brother. He has a brother. Can you keep Johann until I figure out what to do?"

"Of course, Ron."

"I'll pay for everything."

"That's fine, Ron. We'll take good care of him. You don't

have to worry. You can pay by check or you can give me a credit card number over the phone."

"Thank you."

"You must have cared about each other."

"We did, Kevin. We were like brothers."

"I can see that. It's touching. We take Visa, MasterCard, American Express, or Diner's Club."

"Now?"

"Whenever it's convenient. But since I have you on the phone…"

I gave Kevin my Visa card number. "Thank you, Ron. And when you contact Johann's brother, will you ask him something and get right back to me?"

"Yes, sure. What?"

"A request for embalming must be signed by a relative. Otherwise, we'll cremate the remains. There's a limited amount of time in which we can wait for a decision. We can keep a body only so long before… Well, at a certain point, it's too late to be embalmed, if you know what I mean."

"I have to go now, Kevin."

I hung up. For the first time, I was struck by the corporeal elements of Johann's death. I'd embraced the fact of his absence, that he was dead and I'd never see him again. But Kevin's polite attempt to step around the gruesome aspects of death—the mortification of tissue—led me to consider the event from a medical point of view. Johann died of a broken neck. Did that guarantee that he died instantly? Or did he lie on the highway staring at the sky, feeling the chilly Nevada night on his face, knowing he was about to die? I imagined the truck that struck him stopping and the driver—Otis—hurrying to Johann's side. Or did Otis keep his distance, waving away traffic? How much time had passed before someone—a policeman, a paramedic—reached Johann, and was he, during that time, unconscious and dead or conscious and painfully alive?

I wept. And I faced a conundrum. I needed to maintain a semialert state in order to find Johann's brother and to proceed with the funeral plans. Yet, in this conscious state, I couldn't escape the torturous, circular thoughts regarding Johann's last moments of life. More booze and drugs would obliterate these intrusive mental images but render me too thickheaded for the work I needed to do.

I slapped my face the way hysterical people are slapped in the movies. "Thanks, I needed that," I said aloud, laughed at my joke, and then slapped my face again, cutting short the laughter. Slapping was effective; it drove useless thoughts from my brain. But I worried about handprints on my face. I would have to venture into the world if I was going to deliver Johann home. Repetitive face-slapping might leave marks. I tried slapping my body's fleshier regions—arms, chest, thighs—but felt no real sting, and without the pain the gesture seemed halfhearted and cowardly. Besides, frequent slapping would occupy my hands; I needed them free for dialing the telephone and writing checks.

I thought of adolescents I'd read about, "cutters," who distance themselves from emotional pain by carving their own limbs; I'd seen photographs of their lacerated forearms. I remembered that my agent had sent me a semicomical Christmas present, a multipurpose tool called a Leatherman (made of stainless steel but encased in leather) that offered several blades of varying lengths and diverse edges. As I searched for the Leatherman among the detritus in my rarely opened toolbox, I reflected that a teenager's solution to incapacitating, psychological turmoil was appropriate for me, in my situation. After all, my feelings for Johann—a relative stranger, the object of projected, overheated fantasies—were akin to a high schooler's crush. I found the knife and unfolded its blades.

I pulled up a sleeve and slashed each blade across the thick part of my forearm, avoiding the veiny section near my wrist; after all, this was not a suicide attempt but an effort to remain alert. The narrow blades cut quickly, leaving a burning after-sensation as the blood rose to the surface of my skin. The feeling was not sharp enough for my purposes. Finally I unfolded a blade with a toothy, serrated edge. Curious, I flipped through the little manual and discovered that this blade was designed for scaling fish. My first attempt to slash my arm with the fish-scaling blade failed; the knife's sharp teeth bounced off my skin. I plied the knife with more pressure, catching skin in the serrated teeth and hauling the blade across my arm. This method worked. The blade caught hold of my skin and rendered it. I howled, but I was alert and calm.

Still, there remained the problem of my arms and my hands left useless, wielding the knife or bleeding. I walked to the bathroom and faced the mirror. I removed my shirt. I applied the fish scaling blade to my chest. The skin here was thicker than the skin of my forearm and required more force. Again I howled, but I found success, leaving a two-inch vertical line above my right nipple. This vertical line by itself seemed pointless, so I turned it into a J with two more gashes and two more howls. Jots of blood dripped into my sink, and I retreated upstairs, finding a black T-shirt to wear to soak up blood while I went to work, determined to find Johann's brother, somewhere in Europe, to break the news to him, to honor his wishes respecting the remains, to send Johann home, and to continue—at necessary intervals—to carve his name across my chest like a kid in junior high school decorating his notebook with the name of a yearned-for upperclassman.

Twenty

I made my first call to Peter, the Czech bodybuilder and Johann's Hollywood roommate, another master who worked out of the "office." The police had notified him of Johann's death.

"What the fuck happened?"

I dissembled, muttering something about "the traffic" and "crowds." But Peter cut me off.

"We know what was this was about." There was a mordant edge to his voice, and I could envision him at work, using that tone on servile clients. "I have a studio apartment. I sleep on the floor next to Johann. Before he left for Vegas, he went into the bathroom every fifteen minutes. His pupils were the size of dimes. How much money did you send him? Didn't you know he'd waste it on drugs?"

"I need to contact his brother. Do you have a phone number for him?"

"Ethan's doing that."

Ethan. Johann had wanted to contact him in the last hour of his life, had tried to dial his number until I snatched the phone from his hands.

"Can I have Ethan's number?"

"Johann was my best friend." *I can take this.* "He always made me laugh at the office. Making fun of the johns. We had a name for every one of them." *Including me?*

"I'm so sorry. I'm going to bury Johann. Next to his mother. I promise. If you'll give me Ethan's number..."

"What am I supposed to do about the rent?"

"Rent...?"

189

"Johann owed me two months' rent."

I remembered how, one evening in Numbers, I referred to the young men working the bar as "escorts." Johann had corrected me. "They're hustlers, Ronnie. Look it up in the dictionary."

I purchased Ethan's telephone number from Peter for a thousand dollars.

I was unprepared for Ethan's masculine, warm voice. "I'm so glad you called. I was worried about you. This must be really hard. I know how much you cared about Johann. Is there anything I can do for you?" With his measured and genuine phrases of sympathy, he sounded like a minister comforting a grieving member of his flock.

"You must hate me."

Ethan had the audacity to laugh. "I'm sure we hate ourselves for different reasons. You blame yourself because you were there when it happened. I blame myself because I wasn't."

"But I *was* there. I could have...*done* something."

"Let's not worry about that. Let's take him home. I've been talking to his brother. They have a family plot. We're going to bury Johann next to his mother and his father." Ethan's voice broke, his strength ebbing. "I've buried *my* mother and father. I can do this..."

"You're an orphan, like Johann."

"That's one of the things we had in common. We'd go to St. Patrick's and light candles for our parents. Johann insisted, every time he came to New York. He was so religious. We've got to have candles for the funeral mass. Lots of candles."

I had trouble picturing Johann kneeling in St. Patrick's. Did he wear his leather jacket and storm-trooper boots? Then I remembered Johann's current state and the inexorable process taking over his body.

"Ethan, we have a decision to make about Johann's..." I

couldn't say the word *remains*. "Future. I'm leaning toward cremation."

"Oh, no." There was a tone of horror in his voice. "We're Catholics. Our bodies have to be buried intact so we can rise from our graves to meet Christ on Judgment Day."

I too had been raised to believe in an apocalyptic meeting with Christ in the sky on Judgment Day, but in a liberal Protestant denomination in which the symbolism of every prophecy was implied.

"Ethan, there's a time factor. Are you sure Johann was a *strict* Catholic?"

"I never saw him when he wasn't wearing his crucifix."

I couldn't picture a crucifix around Johann's neck; perhaps my attention had been directed to other regions. "Johann didn't care about ritual; he was…" I stopped short of calling Johann an "outlaw." It didn't seem like a good idea, considering our last few hours together and the way he died. "He didn't play by the rules. Consider how he made his living."

"You mean, as a personal trainer? What's that have to do with anyone's religion?"

Personal trainer? Was that some sort of code for Johann's profession, the way he and I called crystal meth "stuff"? In light of Ethan's preference for embalming and burial, I found myself lobbying for cremation. This was turning into a turf war.

"Think of transporting him, Ethan. How do you get a coffin onto a plane?"

"I'm sure it's done all the time."

"But think how much simpler it will be if we carry Johann in…"

"An *urn*?"

"It's a long flight to Germany."

There was a pause. "You mean Hungary."

"Johann's from Germany." I tried to sound sure. After all, Johann and I had been so close. Hadn't we?

Ethan's tone was lighter, with a touch of triumph. "Johann is Hungarian. I've been speaking to his brother all morning. He's from a town three hours north of Budapest. I can't pronounce the name of the town. It's got, like, nine syllables. You thought Johann was from Germany?"

"I meant Hungary." I felt myself sinking. If I wasn't Johann's closest confidant, what was I? At least *I* knew how Johann made his living. "Was Johann really your personal trainer?"

"No," Ethan answered, clearing a sob from his throat. "He was the love of my life."

I conceded all to Ethan: embalming, candles, anything he wanted, even mummification or a funeral pyre if they would bring consolation. Ethan suggested we split responsibilities: He would stay in contact with Johann's brother, making arrangements on the Hungarian side, while I worked with the Las Vegas mortuary and booked air travel. Both of us planned to fly to Budapest on the same plane that would carry Johann in his coffin.

The first order of business brought the first hitch to our plans. We needed written permission from Johann's brother, Gabor (the most common of Hungarian names), to embalm Johann. Time was essential, and the document had to be faxed, but no one in Gabor's town owned a fax machine. I called a friend of a friend, an American woman who had married a Hungarian with an office in Budapest. They agreed to receive the fax, and Ethan notified Gabor: He should travel to Budapest, sign the document, and fax it back to the mortuary. As Budapest was eight hours ahead of Las Vegas, the window of opportunity for this transaction was restricted to a ninety-minute period on the following business day. And the three-hour drive from Gabor's town to Budapest had to be factored into the arrangements.

Ethan sounded shaky when he called to report trouble.

Gabor had started talking to a lawyer and refused to proceed until some questions were answered. "He says he doesn't know who we are. He says we're just strangers." Ethan's voice was rising, approaching tears. "He kept saying, 'How do I know you were really friends with Tamas?'"

"Who's Tamas?" I imitated Ethan's pronunciation, with the accent on the second syllable.

"That's Johann's real name."

"Johann's name is Thomas?"

"Tamas Janos Geletly."

I got lost in the memory of Johann standing before me in the dim light of the hustler bar on the night we met, his eyes scouring the room, evaluating, dismissing, calculating, then settling his gaze on me and answering—in his own good time—the first question I ever asked him, his name.

"He *has* to believe us. All we're trying to do is bury his brother."

"That's what I told him. Even Olga became impatient. She was scolding him on the phone, saying, 'How can you doubt the kindness of these men? All they want to do is bring your brother home.'"

Again I was lost. "I'm sorry, Ethan. But who's Olga?"

"Olga is the AT&T translator. She's gotten emotionally involved."

I glanced at the clock. It was ten in the morning, New York time. My friend's Hungarian office would close in an hour. "Is Gabor in Budapest?"

"No. He's at home."

That was it. We had lost a business day. I thought of Johann on a steel table in a refrigerated room. I wondered about the temperature of that room, if it matched the temperature outside my house, if I might experience what Johann was experiencing if I stepped outside in my underwear and lay beneath the hickory tree on crusty snow.

"Gabor says he wants to talk to someone official."

I cringed. I didn't want Gabor speaking to Mr. Frankel of the Las Vegas coroner's department, with his suspicions of Johann's suicidal intentions. I thought of Kevin, the soft-voiced undertaker. "What about the people from the mortuary? They could explain the situation."

"No." Ethan was in turmoil. "He wants to speak to the Hungarian ambassador."

"The Hungarian ambassador? To the *United States*?"

"That's what he said."

I lost my temper. "This is crazy! We don't have time for this. Johann can't be kept on ice forever. I'm sorry, Ethan, we're going to have to cremate him."

Ethan broke; he held the phone away, but I could hear his hiccups of sorrow.

"Okay! No cremation! I'll take care of it! I promise!"

I hung up, entered the bathroom, removed my black T-shirt, which stuck to the scabs on my chest, and stared at the J I'd carved there, melodramatically and inaccurately. I tried—with the fish-scaling knife—to convert the J to a T with three or four vertical slashes. The revision was barely successful, but at least the pain rendered me starkly alert. I put on my T-shirt, returned to the kitchen, and dialed information for Manhattan, asking for the number of the Hungarian consulate. I dialed the number and was put off by a secretary until I mentioned a dead Hungarian. I was put through to the consul, Dr. Sandor Vargas. I laid out my dilemma and waited for his reply.

Dr. Vargas's voice was dour, the tone of a man who was infrequently surprised. "I'm sorry. I don't know what you expect me to do."

"Talk to Gabor. He needs to hear from someone official, someone Hungarian."

"What would I say?"

"Tell him we're just trying to bury Tamas (I thought it good strategy to use his real, Hungarian name). We don't have any hidden agendas. We were his best friends. Just assure Gabor that our intentions are good. Ethan and I need you to vouch for us."

Dr. Vargas used my first name, a portent—I was learning—of bad news. "Ron, the problem is, I don't have any idea who you are."

I burst into tears. It had not been calculated, but it won the day. Dr. Vargas acquiesced. "Send your friend—what is his name? Ethan?—to my office. Make sure he has proper identification. I'll speak to the young man in Hungary. I'll tell him..." Dr. Vargas paused. "I'll tell him something. You've got a funeral to plan, don't you?"

"Yes, yes" I blubbered. "In some town north of Budapest. A long name, with nine syllables."

"Satoraljaujhely." Dr. Vargas murmured the name of Johann's town with a hint of wistfulness, like a funeral prayer; it was so long, in another language he might have been speaking a complete sentence.

According to Ethan, Dr. Vargas spoke for a good ten minutes to Gabor, in Hungarian, after which Gabor relented and apologized. Documents were exchanged so that Johann could be "processed."

When I notified Kevin, the Las Vegas mortician, that the appropriate papers would be eking out of his fax machine at any moment, he sounded exasperated, despite his sotto voce, funeral-parlor tone, "I have to warn you, Ron..." (again, the first name) "...we're at the very edge of an acceptable time limit for embalming."

"What does that mean, in practical terms?"

"Keep the casket closed."

With Johann "stabilized," the funeral was planned for the third week of January, and I concentrated on my share of the tasks at hand. Johann's belongings had been returned to his apartment in Los Angeles, and Peter agreed to relinquish them, free of charge. He was glad to hear I was taking Johann's things to Hungary, to hand them over to Johann's brother. I let him keep the storm-trooper boots.

"Did you know Johann's real name was Tamas?" I couldn't resist asking.

"Oh, sure. I called him Tommy all the time." He pronounced "Tommy" with a long "o," as in "owe me."

"Did everyone know?" I was trying to calculate my place in Johann's world.

"Just his friends. Not his clients."

I made travel arrangements. I received daily reports from Ethan on the progress of the funeral plans. There would be a mass, as well as a graveside service, roses and music, a choral piece by Handel.

"Fine, fine. Whatever you want. Ethan? Did you call Johann 'Johann' or 'Tamas'?"

Ethan answered and I imagined him smiling, enjoying the memory. " 'Johann', most of the time. 'Tommy' when I wanted to get his attention. Do you want to know what he called me? 'Cio-Cio-San.' Do you know what that means?"

"It sounds vaguely familiar."

Ethan chuckled. "At first I thought it was Hungarian. Some endearment. It sounded so cute. Most of the time he shortened it, to Cio-Cio. 'Bye-bye, Cio-Cio. How are you, Cio-Cio?' One night I saw the opera *Madama Butterfly*. I almost fell out of my seat. Cio-Cio-San is the name of the main character, the Japanese geisha who falls in love with an American soldier. He leaves her. She commits harry-karry."

"Hara-kiri," I corrected. I had seen a lot of Japanese films.

The conversation dropped to silence as I contemplated Cio-Cio-San's fate. I was familiar with the climactic aria from *Madama Butterfly*, "Un bel di." The geisha waits foolishly for her lover to return, one fine day; she envisions him cresting the hill, heading home. I glanced out the window to my front yard, to the driveway that approaches my house, rising to a small hill before it disappears among the trees. The snow was packed and ashened, and the sun was giving up for the day, relinquishing the sky to gray and, farther away, navy blue. Never would Johann walk down that hill, toward my home, and besides, his name wasn't Johann. And I was no flamboyant, operatic figure. I was a middle-aged man who had loved a hustler; I was moderately successful in my work, abjectly lonely, probably alcoholic, certainly drug-addicted, self-absorbed, pathetically grandiose, but not without a sense of my own ridiculousness. "I'm not a tragic heroine." Realizing I'd said it aloud, I giggled. "But I play one on television."

"Ron?" Ethan put on his young minister's voice, chafing my nerves. "Are you all right?"

Was I all right? I had no answer to that question. There was, I imagined, such a thing as "all right" in this minute, as far as the basics of life were concerned: I was breathing, I was standing, I was holding the telephone. I realized that my free hand was tugging relentlessly on a clump of my hair. The hand seemed to be operating outside of my control, with its own private motivations. I could feel some of the hairs popping from my scalp. I knew I was close to screeching but for some reason was not screeching. My hand, my hair, my scalp, and my mouth seemed to exist on different planes of feeling, as if I had turned into a Cubist self-portrait.

"I'm fine, Ethan. I have to go now."

I hung up the telephone intending to commit hara-kiri.

Twenty-One

My attempt at hara-kiri was a halfhearted experiment.

I was curious to know if I was the kind of person who *could* kill himself if it came to that, to encounter the moment that Johann encountered and stumbled through when he stood on the shoulder of a freeway in Las Vegas and saw a truck approaching. If Johann had committed suicide, as Mr. Frankel suggested, what were the seconds and half-seconds like as he waited for the truck before ordering his feet to step forward? I sought at least to bring myself to that climactic juncture. Then I would choose to proceed or draw back.

First I ensured that my responsibilities had been discharged in case the experiment succeeded. (Don't people speak of a "successful" suicide as one that ends in death?) My dogs would be cared for: I had stipulations in my will for that. My house would go to a friend with two young children. The mortuary in Las Vegas had my credit card number, as did my travel agent, who was handling the transport of Johann to Hungary. No matter where my experiment led, Johann would go home, accompanied by Ethan who loved him better and truer, and at least knew his real name.

I collapsed into a kitchen chair when I thought of my parents and the pain I would cause them if I managed to kill myself. They were the only people who really depended on me. Not that others didn't care. Plenty of people cared, in the sense that plenty of people felt affection toward me and would miss me if I died.

But my parents relied on me in specific ways. I arranged trips for them to Florida. I confronted Medicare representatives over inappropriate charges. And I think I gave them a reason to live. I was a source of adventure, with my exotic friends and—to them—bizarre tastes. With me, they had ridden in limousines, stayed in hotels, seen a puppet play in a cave, wandered—stupefied—through modern art museums, met movie stars, and tasted sushi. Once I got my mother drunk on champagne and she fell down the stairs of my Greenwich Village apartment building, hands splayed in front of her, skimming the steps like a cartoon figure. She was unscathed except for one bruise. The event became legendary. We couldn't get through a single meal without recounting it until my mother's brain began to die and she became a sullen hoarder of chocolate bars, someone without memories and with no capacity for laughter.

This image of my mother—sitting on the edge of a bed, gazing stupidly at a blank television, gorging cashews from a wrinkled paper sack—gave me the impetus to proceed with my experiment. Her annihilation, my father's slow expiration (mirroring Gloria's), and Johann's violent, psychotic end seemed all of one piece: a Chinese menu of demise. In this context, my (potential) termination at the end of a bloody knife seemed natural, another item from the menu or perhaps the evening's special. Before I changed my mind again, I headed to the bathroom with the multipurpose, many-bladed tool called the Leatherman.

The first thing I learned about hara-kiri is that it isn't easy. Puncturing the skin of the abdomen—my abdomen, at least—requires more than ordinary pressure, a plunge rather than the steady force I applied with one of the Leatherman's sharpest blades. I had been able to rend the skin of my chest and arms with determined slashes, but I couldn't pierce my belly with the point of the sharp knife, although I left a stark indentation midway between my sternum and navel, like a ding on a car after a parking lot mishap. Contrary to the hallucinations I'd suffered in Las Vegas regarding the fragility of my skin, I found that while my skin yielded to laceration, it remained obdurate against plunging and piercing. Frustrated, I retreated to the kitchen, where I found my dogs whining at the back door, begging to be released, an indication that my Mishima-like efforts in the bathroom had been accompanied by wailing. I opened the door and my shepherd mixes bolted into the January afternoon.

I filled a glass with liquor. Each action seemed significant, as it was (potentially) leading toward a final one. I placed a Vicodin on the kitchen table and studied it, flicking my thumb against the place where the halves of the capsule had been joined, admiring its plastic lamina, which held firm against my fingers but promised to dissolve in the juices of my stomach. It seemed a marvelous invention, the capsule, and I wondered if I really wanted to leave a world in which such innovations were possible, in which God's hand working through evolution had created, from an amoeba through frogs and gorillas and Neanderthals and Visigoths and Huns, the kind of enlightened being that could invent a *capsule*. Viewing the capsule as the end product of human progress, I placed six of them into my mouth without reservation; it seemed, in fact, an ennobling gesture.

I had never put six capsules into my mouth before, so I held them on my tongue and considered the experience. It was a half-step toward suicide, perhaps a quarter-step or one-eighth step. I was not frightened. I washed down the pills with port wine, drinking from my favorite, Depression-era tumbler, savoring the cool, nostalgic feelings aroused by the cobalt blue glass, memories of my grandmother's china closet and wandering among tables at flea markets on summer afternoons. Fearing a derailment from my mission, I swallowed the rest of the Vicodin, seven capsules, in a group of four, then a group of three, inadequate for death but sufficient for a preparation for death, a slow engagement with the cold water of mortality in the shallow end of the pool.

"Now what?" I spoke aloud. "This is weird, but I'm bored. Is this the final irony? That suicide is *boring*?"

I tried scribbling a note to my parents, an apology, but my hand drifted onto the counter, smearing ink. I set to cleaning the counter, pondering the proper treatment for the polyurethaned wood, stumped with a choice between a scouring powder and a pine-scented wood polish, which led me to question my fastidiousness at such a moment. Somehow, during this quandary, I fell to the kitchen floor.

"I'm on the floor. I don't remember falling. I wonder if my head is bleeding. No, no blood. I wonder, if I slam my head against the floor, if I can *make* it bleed. Ouch! Fuck, that hurt. Am I bleeding now? No. Shit. I don't bleed very easily. My skin is airtight. Maybe I'm not pounding it hard enough. Am I afraid of the pain? *Pound your head against the floor, you fucking coward!* Ouch! Damn! Shit! Fuck! This fucking hard floor! Am I...? No. Not bleeding! I'm bulletproof. I'm chain mail. Get up. Take more pills. Crawl if you can't stand. Crawl to the bathroom. Get up. Open the medicine chest. Yes, Master. I'm opening it, Master. Yes, Master, there are pills in there. Jesus, like a million pills. What am I, some kind of invalid? Zouvirax. I don't think it will kill me. But at least my corpse won't have herpes. Ha, ha! What else? Seldane. Paxil. Prescription Benadryl. Full bottle. Like forty of them. 'One at night for sleeping.' Pretty capsule. Pink and white. Who chooses the colors of capsules? It's someone's *job*. Yes, Master. I'm opening the bottles, Master. What would you have done, Johann, if I had held on to you that night? Six pills, a handful. Swallow them. Yes, Master. What would have happened if I had made you stay in the room with me? If I had said, 'No, don't go out there, by yourself. Stay here. I'll take care of you?' Yes, Master, more pills. All of them? Yes, I'm putting all of them into my hand. Swallow them? Now, Master? All right. I've swallowed. More? Yes, Master. I'll swallow... There. More. The rest? All right. I mean, Yes, Master. I'll swallow all of..."

I emptied the bottle into my hand, then my mouth. I crawled from the bathroom to the kitchen and into the dining room, which was dark and womb-like, paneled with walnut wainscoting. Here I kept my collection of Christian-themed art, gathered during my travels and mounted as an homage to my churchgoing youth. I studied ceramic holy water fonts from Mexico, a carved wooden Nativity from Puerto Rico, a Polish Madonna in molded silver. I turned away from the Madonna, as I could not bear her scrutiny, but found myself observed by the subject of my favorite artifact, Saint Lucy, captured in an oil painting, a flea market find. Saint Lucy is legendary for having *two* sets of eyes, the pair in her head that had grown back—a miracle!—after being gouged and two more on a plate in her hand. I sensed reproach in the quartet of Saint Lucy's eyes.

Jesus was represented in agony on every wall, hanging from Brazilian crucifixes and Roman rosaries, including one made of pewter from the Vatican and blessed by the pope. His palms were pierced by nails, his head by thorns. I remembered a weekend retreat I had attended as a teenager, sponsored by Youth for Christ, in which a mournful counselor—a reformed gangster with a drooping black mustache and a mafioso's blunt style—had passed a box of nails among the crowd and asked us to press the point of the nail against our palms while he described Christ's crucifixion, flogging, and impaling with an anatomical exactitude that implied real-life experience with human flesh and its reaction to sharpened instruments. I thought of the teenage cutters who scored their forearms with razors and their liberation through suffering. I imagined Johann on a barren Las Vegas freeway, writhing in the wretchedness of a lonely, imminent death.

Finally I understood the reproach in Saint Lucy's eyes: I was *not* suffering. I lay on the clean floor of a warm house surrounded by souvenirs and upscale furnishings, anesthetized by pain-suppressing medication. The torment of

Jesus, Saint Lucy, Johann, and faceless boys and girls with lacerated limbs beckoned to me, and it became perfectly clear what I ought to do.

I pulled on my boots, dug through my toolbox for a pair of wire clippers, and headed for the backyard. The previous owners had kept horses, and a remnant of their captivity—a length of barbed wire—ran along several trees. I clipped six feet of barbed wire from the onetime horse fence and returned to my house. I carried the wire to my bedroom, where I stripped to my Jockey shorts. I wrapped the wire around my torso, the barbed points pressing into my skin, and secured the wire with strips of gaffer's tape, left over from my days as a film student.

Glistening in silver from my nipples to my belly button like a reflective half-mummy and with nothing better to do, I lay on the floor of my television room—with the windows open, to simulate the temperature of a morgue—and flicked through the television's channels. I stopped on Nickelodeon, which was featuring an *Avengers* festival. I was amused when Emma Peel appeared in a scene dressed similarly to myself, in a zippered skintight silver Mylar suit.

Twenty-Two

For those wishing to replicate Christ's suffering and mortification, I'm here to say there must be methods more effective than fixing a section of horse fence to your torso with years-old gaffer's tape that has lost its power to adhere.

I waited for unconsciousness, but it didn't come. The gusting wind caused a loose wire—cable television or telephone—to whack against a window, and I focused on the repetitive sound, picturing the cable, tracing it, counting the "taps" in batches of ten, conjuring a musical accompaniment, a song by Patti Smith with a haranguing bending of a single word, coordinating the word to the rhythm of the detached, undulating wire, "Now-ow-ow-ow-ow-ow-ow-ow-ow-ow."

I began to doubt if death was guaranteed by the combination of substances I'd swallowed. There wafted among my thoughts the prospect of debilitating brain injury, requiring wheelchairs, respirators, and round-the-clock nurses. I listened to my breathing and imagined it produced by a machine (the tapping of the loose wire on the window became the pulsing of the mechanism). I contemplated my arms paralyzed, my legs lifeless. I projected the feel of a spoon in my mouth, the taste of pureed fruit and the humiliation of being fed by minimum-wage health care aides wearing discordantly cheerful flower-print uniforms. I considered the smell of urine and the experience of sitting in one's own feces waiting to be changed. I conjured diapers. I pictured them in stacks around me, as they were stacked in my mother's bedroom. I envisioned their plastic packaging, the gauzy diapers themselves, in pastels, infantilizing pink and baby blue.

I turned off the television and lay still, imagining the end of consciousness, when I would think about nothing, remember nothing. I struggled not to move, not a limb, even to prohibit my chest from rising and falling. I concentrated on the points of barbed wire poking my ribs; I felt irritation but no real pain. In fact, my makeshift hair shirt was counterproductive. as it induced restlessness rather than drowsiness. A spot in the middle of my back—beneath the gaffer's tape—began to itch.

I stripped away the gaffer's tape (the tape pulling on my body hair was the deepest pain I'd managed to inflict upon myself so far) and unwound the barbed wire, yielding to retreat. I had faced my "Johann" moment, my "standing on the side of a highway with a truck coming" moment. And I had flinched. I was going to do for myself what I did not do for Johann. I moved slowly, as some part of me hoped to faint before concluding this act of surrender. I crept to the telephone. I punched in a number, pausing significantly between each digit, giving fate a chance to intervene. I called Armand, my carpenter friend who raised peculiar, inedible chickens, and blurted, when he answered, "I just swallowed a bunch of pills."

"Why?" he asked.

Armand drove me to the hospital in his truck, where he spent a great deal of time, if the debris at my feet was any indication: crumb-filled sandwich bags; discarded packets of soy sauce; flat, curved sticks from consumed frozen yogurt bars; and scattered rind of clementines.

He drove without urgency, slowing at yellow traffic lights. He seemed unimpressed with my suicide attempt, but he was never rattled by death or its prospect. Once he had come to a dinner party at my house wearing his deceased mother-in-law's chemotherapy wig, explaining, "My head was cold." He revered Chinese pheasants and Indian ducks but regarded the end of life with a farmer's lack of sentimentality.

"I came close to blowing my head off with a Saturday night special." He recounted the darkest days of his depression—when he lived alone, before he fell in love with Caroline—in a Prozac-regulated monotone. "When I get depressed, more than usual, I get totally lethargic. I don't *move*. And one day, a couple of winters ago, I was standing in my yard staring at nothing, just the sky, and a black-capped chickadee landed on my head. I mean, it roosted on my head. That's how depressed I was—I was still as a post."

Armand had retreated to his house—once the chickadee flew away—and wept, finally pointing a pistol to his temple.

"Why didn't you shoot?"

"Why did you call me?"

We drove the rest of the way in silence.

I shuffled into the emergency room behind Armand. He consulted with a burly triage nurse who planted herself in my path.

"What happened to you, sir?"

"I had an accident."

She wrapped a meaty hand around my arm and said, "Come with me," and I learned what happens when you tell a no-nonsense, night shift, emergency room triage nurse to go fuck herself.

"Security!"

Within seconds I was spread-eagled on a gurney, with off-duty police officers pinning my arms, while the triage nurse slathered one of my nostrils with Vaseline. A nurse's aide applied Vaseline to the end of a tube, five feet long, with the circumference—from my point of view, at least—of a garden hose.

"What's that for?"

"We pump liquid charcoal into your stomach. It sucks up the poison. Then we pump it out. Then we do it again."

I was flummoxed by the geography. "But the tube goes…?"

"Up your nose, down your throat, and into your stomach."

"Over the river and through the woods." I made her smile. The aide unbuttoned my shirt and the triage nurse lost her smile, gaping at my chest, where I had carved a J and then tried to revise it into a T with the serrated edge of a fish-scaling knife.

"You're having an interesting evening," the nurse said.

A resident arrived, and Armand showed him the empty prescription bottles he had collected from my floor. The resident was Hispanic, stocky, with a shaved head and an earring. He snapped his gum and rocked on his heels, as if he had overdosed on caffeine. Coldly, he studied my body carvings. He glanced at a chart and mispronounced my name. He grilled me concerning the number of pills I'd swallowed and the amount of alcohol I'd consumed. I felt people at my feet, tugging off my shoes. I felt other hands pricking me with needles. I saw I.V. tubes dangling from translucent sacks on metal poles. I kept my eye on the greased tube as another aide attached it to something that looked like a microwave oven, on a cart with wheels. I felt faint. The lights burned brighter, the faces of the people surrounding me dimmed, and I began to lose the ability to connect voices to faces. The resident jammed the tube up my nose, and I cursed him until the tube entered my throat and gagging rendered cursing impossible.

After some hours in the emergency room, ingesting and regurgitating liquid charcoal, courtesy of the belching compressor, I was admitted to a regular room.

My arms were strapped to the bed rails to prevent me from dislodging the I.V. lines. Although the stomach pump had been disconnected, the tube remained, dangling from my nose. When the day shift nurse came on duty I told her my name was Babar.

"Well, my name is Larene. You let me know if there's anything you need."

Larene's skin was coal-black, and she wore her hair in cornrows studded with beads that clicked.

"Can you take this tube out of my nose?"

Larene checked my chart. "I don't see any orders to have it removed."

My head ached, with my sinuses adhering to the tube. "I don't see the point of keeping it in. If you've pumped my stomach. If it's *been* pumped…"

Larene patted my hand. "Maybe they're planning to pump it some more. Maybe you put *so much* poison into your system they're just going to pump and pump for Lord knows *how* much longer."

My roommate was large and ashen; his hospital gown couldn't contain the wads of gray flesh. With his hand poised on the controls of the single television that hung between our beds, he asked in a weary voice, "Do you object to professional wrestling?"

"Philosophically, no. Maybe on an aesthetic level."

He never spoke to me again.

Just as I had second thoughts about killing myself, I was suffering second (third?) thoughts about *not* killing myself. My interior soliloquies were circular, self-pitying, and exasperating, along the lines of: *I don't deserve to live, but I don't have the courage to kill myself, which makes me even less worthy to live.* These reflections intensified as the hours passed, with my mind becoming hyperalert thanks to the professional vacuuming my system had received. This mental clarity was not welcome; I yearned for stupor. But the doctors denied my requests for painkillers, even aspirin.

"I don't see any orders for medication," Larene trilled in a singsong voice I came to identify as faux-sympathetic. "I guess they figure you already took *enough* drugs."

Despite my revived mental acuity—and nothing to do but lie on my back and think—I collected no epiphanies, only emptiness and doubt.

Larene followed me the few steps to the bathroom, guiding the wheeled stand that supported the bags of fluids and tangles of tubes that were attached to my arms. She revealed, in the first hours of our relationship, that she was a deaconess of her church and a sometimes substitute preacher. She was proud of a particular sermon her flock clamored to hear.

"It is about fear." She spelled it out. "F.E.A.R. Do you know what that stands for? False Evidence Appearing Real. Like you have evidence that God does not love you. Like you have *evidence* that life is not worth living. But this evidence is not real. It is in your *mind.*" Apparently, when Larene fell into her preaching mode, she stopped using contractions. "But your mind has the ability to make these false things appear to you to be real." She drew out the last, key words of each sentence, "fear," "mind," "real," adding breath to her voice, propelling her words through the air to me, her captive audience.

I suffered a lecture from the resident who had been on duty when I arrived in the emergency room. Apparently, I had skated close to mortality, as forty Benadryl *are* sufficient to cause death.

"Your heart might have stopped at any moment." He snapped his fingers for emphasis. "Or you might have slipped into unconsciousness before getting help. Or you might have fallen and bumped your head, knocking yourself out. Or you might have fallen into a deep sleep and choked on your own vomit. Or…"

He reminded me of a waiter at a restaurant with too many specials on the menu. I cut him off. "It was an accident. I didn't want to die."

"I'm thinking of sending you to the psych unit. Have you ever seen a psychiatrist?"

I attempted my most reasonable-sounding voice. "Only for research. A couple of years ago I was working on a script for Jodie Foster about schizophrenia." The resident's eyes widened. I realized I might be sounding delusional. "It's true. I'm a

Hollywood screenwriter. I know everyone claims to be a screen-writer these days. I bet *you're* working on a screenplay."

The resident ran his hands over the lacerations on my arms and poked at the letters carved into my chest, checking, he said, for infection. He refused to discharge me or remove the tube from my nose. In fact, he prescribed another dose of liq-uid charcoal. A compressor was wheeled into the room and I endured another stomach-pumping session. My roommate sat on the edge of his bed facing me, taking in the procedure, eating potato chips.

I planned to leave, with or without a doctor's discharge.
"What about those I.V. lines?" Larene was skeptical. "You expect me to follow you down the street, pushing that stand?"
"I'll pull them out."
"You gonna pull out that *tube*?"
I wrapped both hands around it and tugged. Immediately I began to gag and surrendered. Larene left the room laughing.

Armand stopped by to assure me that my dogs were being fed and walked.
"Would you pull this tube out of my nose? I can't do it. I just want to go home."
Armand answered "No" and left.

My jumbo roommate's copious wife gaped at me in horror.
"Just pull out this tube. The doctors don't care. They're not using it. They're just leaving it in to make some kind of statement."
She waddled to her husband's side of the room and yanked the privacy curtain closed. I never saw her leave. She must have crept past after I fell asleep.

I confronted a young woman in green scrubs. "They've fin-ished pumping my stomach. Just grab hold and pull."

"Mister," she pleaded, "I'm not a doctor. I'm maintenance. I clean."

"For God's sake, you don't need a medical degree. Please!"

I never saw her again.

Larene entered my room at the beginning of her shift at 5:30 A.M. She stood as a silhouette in the doorway, holding something in her hands. It might have been my chart or it might have been a Bible.

"Suicide is a sin," she proclaimed. "Do you want to know why?"

"A…" I launched into an alphabetical list of complaints. "I might have been asleep. And B…"

"Suicide is a sin because it is selfish."

"It's against the law for you to preach religion to me."

"The *law*?" She lobbed the word across the darkened room. "What're you gonna do? Have me *arrested*?"

On the third morning of my hospital stay, I plucked the I.V. lines from my arms. My hands had been freed from the bed rails within hours of my being admitted, by Larene, muttering something about "patients' rights."

It was early morning. My roommate was snoring. The television lit the room with flickering images, and the sound played, tinny and remote, from a speaker built into his bed. The hospital corridor was quiet, with the midnight shift waiting for relief. I intended to leave the hospital, hail a cab on the street, and find my way home. It was not too late to go to Hungary with Ethan and Johann, but I wasn't sure I could bear it. I yearned to sink into my own bed and pull the covers over my head.

I peeled away tape and gripped the exposed section of a catheter, easing the submerged needle from vein and skin. A drop of blood appeared at the site of removal. For some reason I dabbed this blood onto my finger and tasted it.

I yanked the I.V. lines from my other arm. I anticipated dressing, skulking out of the hospital, and dealing with the tube hanging from my nose in due course. I believed I could manage it. After all, I *had* wrapped myself in barbed wire.

Beneath my mental plans for heading home, retreating to my bed, and sinking to sleep beneath an heirloom quilt, another plan took shape. In this second plan, I would take a taxi to Poughkeepsie, to a cop spot, locate a dealer, buy crack or powdered cocaine (this plan required a detour to an ATM), return home with the drugs and "party." The self-destructive quality of this plan was so evident that my stomach flipped; still, I couldn't banish it from my thoughts. As if embarrassed, I held this plan submerged beneath the first, like a set of transparencies used by teachers for classroom presentations, with images from each plan alternating in my mind's eye: my bed, my grandmother's quilt, my dogs, the familiar cop spot, a line of coke splayed across my glass-topped nightstand.

It seemed as if two people were using the same brain and one of them had the louder, public voice and declaimed unreliable—but sincere—intentions, while the other spoke in a whisper, but always the truth. It was my intention—really—to go home to sleep. Yet I *knew* the chances of going directly home, without a rerouting to Poughkeepsie to cop drugs, were small, since the idea had presented itself. I may struggle to cling to my original intentions, to blot out the second plan with the first, but the outcome remained murky, a toss-up. From the moment the idea of copping and using drugs entered my mind I was beholden to it.

Afraid to venture from the hospital, to test this theory, I lay on my bed gaping at the muted television. The I.V. lines hung useless past my bed, catheters pointing to the floor, and remained so for several hours, with staff coming and going, delivering and reclaiming a breakfast tray, checking my temperature, and inquiring about my insurance plan.

Dr. Yu found me. "Lucky coincidence," he said. "I have another patient on this floor." He took in my scarred chest and arms and opened his hands to the ceiling, as if praying. "Why did you do such a stupid thing to yourself?"

I raised my arms and dropped them to the bed, imitating a sign of resignation I'd learned from my father.

"How long have you been here?"

"Two days. And a half."

"Did you tell them to call me?"

I shook my head.

"You *didn't*?" Dr. Yu sighed an injured exhalation. "Huh? I thought we had a good relationship."

I tried to comfort him. "You were helpful."

"No. I think we made very small progress."

"That's not true. I learned a lot."

"No, no. I don't think I did you any good." Dr. Yu grasped the side rails, exasperated. His reaction seemed over-the-top, raising the possibility that it was staged. Still, I fought against an urge to place my hand over his, the way Larene had covered my hand during our first encounter.

"It's not a classroom," he declaimed. "For me to teach you this fact and that fact about yourself. These lessons are a by-product of the process. The important thing is the process, which is not an adequate word—kind of an ugly word—in English, but sounds much better in Chinese." He spoke the Chinese word for process: *fu*. "In *fu* there must be trust. It's professional but has some elements of a friendship. But you and I... That never happened. We were always removed from each other. You must admit this is true. After all, you did not request me when you were admitted. This is significant. Yes, patients come and go. You get attached to them and they disappear. But you think if they get into trouble, they will call. At least, if someone asks, 'Do you have a doctor?' they will give your name."

My failure seemed complete: I had let down my psychiatrist. "I don't think you should take it personally, Dr. Yu. I'm kind of 'removed' from everybody."

"Huh? What about the drugs? Are you an addict?" That was a sucker punch, presented so casually I was duped into honesty.

"I think so."

"Huh? Alcoholic?"

"I think so."

"Huh? You want to go to rehab?"

"Does anybody *want* to go to rehab?"

"It's either rehab or meetings, your choice."

I dreaded those meetings: church basements, metal chairs, holding hands. But I had been paralyzed, afraid to leave the hospital, convinced of my inability to fulfill any plan without a derailment to bars, liquor stores, prostitutes, and crack dens. Not to mention fish-scaling knives and barbed wire. I wondered if I would ever tell Dr. Yu about the barbed wire. Would our *fu* take us all the way to the barbed wire?

Dr. Yu offered incentive: "There's always the second floor."

"The locked ward?"

"Double-locked," he said, with an eerie, meaningful smile.

"You can't send me there against my will."

"Hu-u-uh?" He drew it out, an exclamation and a challenge. "Look at your arms. Look at your chest. Look at the tube hanging out of your nose. Who do you think goes to the second floor and how do you think they get there? They just walk in?"

I agreed to attend some meetings. We negotiated the number. He wanted me to attend thirty. I was willing to attend one. We settled on six. And I would report to him every day. And for at least a week I would stay with a friend or invite a friend to stay in my house; I would avoid being alone at night.

What about Hungary? Johann was scheduled to be transported in two weeks. My seat, next to Ethan's, had been purchased. There were plans yet to be executed. I was sure to find messages on my answering machine from Ethan, the Las Vegas mortuary, my travel agent, a Hungarian friend who was translating a poem for Johann's funeral.

I told Dr. Yu about Johann's death and the plans to bury him next to his mother in his hometown north of Budapest. I recounted our fatal days in Las Vegas. I described my imagined heart attack and the way Johann had rubbed my chest with Vicks VapoRub, swirling the salve over my skin, murmuring calm assurances until I recaptured my breath. I wept telling this part of the story, not so much with grief, but for the beauty of the moment, the perfect generosity of Johann's gesture. I had cried over Johann in the past, but always at the end of a binge. In front of Dr. Yu, I wept for Johann without the stimulation of chemicals, which had been purged by the disconnected, no-longer-detested stomach pump.

Twenty-Three

For a good hour I lay there prostrate beside her corpse. Then I recollected that Carmen had often told me that she would like to lie buried in a wood. I dug a grave for her with my knife and laid her in it.

—Prosper Merimee, Carmen

I prepare a journal to carry to Hungary, including poems of mourning and photos of Johann from our sunny week in Key West, with him posing behind the wheel of a Mustang convertible and the two of us sailing at sunset, his arm crooked over my neck.

At JFK, I locate a designated counter and check that Johann has made the connection from Las Vegas. A service representative telephones "Pete" in "cargo" and asks if he has "loaded any human remains."

Ethan arrives. I'm surprised by his handsomeness, with broad shoulders and wavy black hair that dangles over his forehead in the manner of 1940s movie stars. He wears a top-coat and Italian shoes. My first words to him are loaded with self-pity: "Can you forgive me?"

He smiles. "Only if you forgive *me.*"

Ethan does not care to hear the details of Johann's death. "I'm sure Johann was doing something he shouldn't." His tone is forbearing, the tone of a long-suffering parent sighing over the latest misdeeds of a delinquent but favored child.

We are accompanied to Budapest by Johann's former roommate, Gabor (not the brother), who will serve as guide and translator. Gabor drags one leg and is scarred from his left eye to his hairline (thanks to a highway smashup that put him into a weeklong coma—his family was gathered around his bedside to say farewell when he opened his eyes and asked, "What happened?"). Unlike Ethan, Gabor is anxious to learn the particulars of Johann's death, and his questions—asides, when Ethan disappears into the men's room—are perceptive, "Was he partying? Do you party?" And then, as if to gain my confidence: "It's okay. I party too."

I remember Johann had refused to introduce me to Gabor or give me his number in New York. "He's dangerous for you, Ronnie." When I tell Gabor about the perplexing location of Johann's accident (perplexing if one discounts a motive of suicide), he offers an alternative theory: "He was heading for a strip club. He loved to watch the strippers when he was high."

We fly Malév Hungarian Airlines. Ethan and I restrict our conversation to innocuous topics: his work (designing high-end office furniture) and mine, recent travels, his New York apartment, my Woodstock farmhouse, his cats, my dogs. We do not skirt the subject of Johann entirely but creep toward it like cautious skaters on a half-frozen pond. Ethan remembers the precise date of his meeting with Johann: May 26, 1994. I recall the month and year of my meeting but not the date. This failure of memory saddens me, and I lapse into silence.

A pal of Gabor's meets us in Budapest; he's been drafted to drive us north, to Johann's hometown. He's introduced with the title "Dr.," although—I learn later—he is a lawyer. He's solidly built, his hair is cropped short in a precise salon cut, and he wears Versace leather pants. His English is perfect, and I ask him to repeat his name. He replies, "You will not be able to pronounce it. Why don't you call me George?"

Two more of Gabor's buddies arrive—Milo and Lazlo—and Ethan and I are sidelined during the boisterous reunion. There's a lot of backslapping and kissing on both cheeks and reminiscing in Hungarian, accompanied by the ringing and answering of cell phones, which are retrieved from belt holsters and pressed to Gabor's ear for more greetings. No one displays—for my taste—the proper attitude of mourning, and I'm not surprised to learn that these young men have never known Johann; this meeting in the airport is Gabor's homecoming.

The entire party travels in two cars to the cargo terminal to see about Johann. Ethan and I ride with George and Gabor in George's Mercedes. George tries to teach us to pronounce his true name: Zsolt. Each of us mangles it. He throws up his hands, launching into a diatribe in Hungarian, with Gabor chiming in enthusiastically.

Ethan whispers to me, "What do you think they're talking about?"

I whisper back, "How do you say 'stupid American faggots' in Hungarian?"

Outside the cargo terminal we search for a hearse but spot only a rusting van, oddly painted baby blue. Gabor assures us this is the vehicle that will transport Johann. Its decrepit appearance validates Gabor's assertion that every Hungarian who lives outside Budapest is an ignorant peasant from the Middle Ages. The funeral director steps out of the van to greet us. At least he bears a reverent attitude. His name is Mr. Budas, and he assures us he will take care of Johann and that Gabor (Johann's brother) will meet us in Mr. Budas's place of business the following morning, when we will finalize details, choose a casket, and order a headstone.

Ethan wishes to form a motorcade to Satoraljaujhely, escorting Johann's casket, lending the three-hour trip an element of ritual. Gabor vetoes that plan, pointing to the baby-blue van and claiming, "It'll take them three *days* to get there." Ethan and I stand at a disadvantage, as we don't speak Hungarian. As everyone climbs into respective vehicles, leaving Mr. Budas to welcome Johann's casket while the rest of us go to breakfast, I say to Ethan, "You realize, don't you, that we are no longer in charge of this event?"

As Zsolt pulls up to a café in Budapest, Gabor grills him: "Is this a good restaurant?"

"No," Zsolt replies. "But it *is* a restaurant."

The five Hungarians take over the place, arranging tables. After ordering, the waitress returns to inform us that there are only twelve eggs on the premises and we will have to share them. For Gabor, this is proof of his country's inadequacy. During the meal he tells a long story in Hungarian, which he illustrates by cupping his hands over imaginary breasts.

I don't mind being ignored, as it gives me an opportunity to ponder. Ethan seems preoccupied as well. I try to picture Johann with these young men, laughing and regaling each other with tales (as far as I can figure) of drunken sexual escapades. I concede the possibility that he had been one of them—a happy, robust straight boy—who got derailed in the United States searching for his fortune. In that scenario I'm not an important figure, just a way station on the route to a terminal misadventure.

We stop at Zsolt's apartment, which is decorated in genuine baroque antiques. When Ethan admires a mahogany prayer bench with an embroidered pad for kneeling, Zsolt claims he uses it for sex. "But," he adds, "I only have sex once a year."

Zsolt and Gabor drive us to the region north of Budapest known as Borsod-Abaujzemplen, on Hungary's border with

Slovakia. I write all the names in my journal, forcing my hosts (I've taken to calling them the Hungarian Playboys) to spell them in English. They sing out each letter, converting the Mercedes into a kindergarten class on wheels. It's a rowdy trip, as everything Ethan and I say spurs the Playboys to spasms of hilarity. The laughter doesn't seem mean-spirited. Intermittently, Gabor rails against his country, crying out, as we roll through each town, "How do people live here?" When I ask him to elaborate, he says, "There's no movie, no place to buy clothes, no place to buy food." I ask what the occupants of the single-story brick-and-stucco homes do for work. "Nothing!" he barks, which seems unjust, as every Hungarian within view is embroiled in some activity: rolling a cart, changing a tire, sweeping the street, or hauling wood.

Johann's village has no inn, so we stop in a larger town, Sarospatak, and check into the Hotel Bodrog, on the river of the same name. It's late afternoon and already dark. The establishment is damp and lifeless, decorated with three or four artificial plants. There is a glass case labeled SOUVENIR that displays bottles of wines, liquors, and aperitifs (souvenirs, I suppose, for alcoholics). Zsolt and Gabor deride the empty dining room, smeared windows, and stone floors, and harass the "staff" when she arrives: a stuttering teenage girl with one eyebrow who apologizes for everything. The Playboys buy a bottle of Unicom—the tequila of Hungary—and lead us to our rooms. We meet for dinner and another round of complaints, but Gabor and Zsolt are drunk, and the insults are delivered with giggles; they manage to make the teenage concierge, now our waitress, smile.

I'm exhausted from the long hours of travel but can't sleep. I walk the streets of Sarospatak, enduring winter drizzle. The town's sewage system is under construction and the sidewalks have been replaced—temporarily, I assume—with ditches carrying foul water. Each house is connected to the street by glistening wood planks, individual drawbridges stretching across the communal moat. The air is filled with the smell of kerosene, burning in stoves behind closed doors. One small grocery is open. I buy a bottle of brandy for the Playboys. So far I've remained abstemious, relying on principles I've learned in the meetings I negotiated with Dr. Yu. I'm not secure in sobriety and will—within a few days—revert to drunkenness. The road to recovery, I learn, is fraught and slippery as the cobblestone streets of Sarospatak on a moist, January night.

At breakfast we're abandoned by the Playboys. Zsolt claims to have business in Budapest and Gabor says the same, although Gabor's eyes are downcast and his hands are stuffed into his pockets, which strikes me as a guilty pose. They don't leave us entirely in the lurch, as they've arranged for a local girl to replace them. Her name is Kitty, with the accent on the second syllable: Kit-*tee*. She is pretty, confident, and fluent in English, and her boyfriend, our new driver, is a long-limbed stud with the ubiquitous name of Gabor. Kitty tells us that her Gabor is able to exchange dollars for Hungarian forints at a very good black-market rate.

Kitty and the new Gabor drive us to Mr. Budas's funeral establishment, a few sheds jammed into the corner of a narrow block. We step into a gloomy passageway and receive a shock: It's lined with coffins, standing vertically, on display.

Gabor—Johann's brother—waits for us in the next room. Everything about this young man is severe: His blue eyes are huge above hollowed cheeks, and his hair is pressed close to his head beneath a sheen of gel. He wears a zippered cloth jacket and a black tie over a clean but worn flannel shirt. His seriousness reminds me of photographs of my turn-of-the-century ancestors, although his darting eyes convey the skittishness of a beaten dog. Certainly there is no trace in this austere young man of the reckless race-car driver Johann had described.

As Ethan and I step into the room, Gabor holds a soldier's posture of parade rest, keeping his hands clasped together behind his back, but tears fill his eyes. It feels natural when I take the boy into my arms. He yields to my embrace and breaks into heartrending sobs. I see—through my own tears—Mr. Budas, Kitty, and her Gabor backing out of the room, although Ethan remains. The moments in which I hold Gabor—perhaps half a minute—are longer, I realize, than ever I held his brother. I step back and watch Ethan and Gabor wrap arms around each other. Ethan is paternal, patting Gabor's back.

The first business of the day has been arranged: Gabor wishes to view his brother's remains. When Kitty translates this plan, I fear for a moment that I will vomit. But there's no time for a reaction as the group heads for Mr. Budas's van. Ethan and I are always a step behind, with Kitty translating over her shoulder. I spend my time in Hungary climbing into and out of vehicles, asking, "Where are we going?"

Johann is waiting for us in the funeral chapel of a cemetery. Everyone is calling Johann his real name, Tamas, and Ethan and I develop a system: When we speak to the Hungarians—Gabor or Mr. Budas, through Kitty—we speak of Tamas, but when we confer with each other we speak of Johann.

The cemetery is guarded by iron gates in a tall monument bearing the word KOZ-TEMETO. The path through the cemetery is gravel and mud, although the graves—in straight lines on a hill, rising from the gate—are covered in snow.

The brick chapel has been painted gray to resemble stone. Johann's casket is standing like the coffins in Mr. Budas's shop and surprises me with its curved shape and silver paint, reminding me of an airplane's fuselage. Someone has entered before us and opened the top half, but—mercifully—nothing is visible but a sheet. I want to run from the room. I keep my equilibrium by staring at the back of Ethan's neck, where a tuft of hair sticks out, perhaps dislodged while riding in the van. I sense that the sheet covering Johann is being lifted, and I play a game, waiting for Ethan's hair to fall into place. If it does, I tell myself, then I must view Johann in his coffin. If, however, the clump of hair retains its delinquent position, I will stare at it, rather than anything else. When Ethan bends closer to the coffin, his hair falls into place and I'm undone. I shift my eyes to the coffin. Johann is a sunken gray specter beneath crinkled plastic. I remember the warning from Kevin, the Las Vegas mortician, about embalming Johann "in the nick of time." I think we missed the nick. Johann's face is shriveled, inhuman, resembling a balloon figure in a parade that has lost half its air. Everyone is weeping, and Mr. Budas—who looks increasingly uncomfortable, as if he has never seen so many tears fall from the eyes of grown men—quickly closes the casket.

Mr. Budas produces—from another plastic bag—the denim jacket and cowboy boots Johann had been wearing when he died (I remember Johann stepping into the boots before leaving our hotel room—I remember his feet in thin black socks sliding into the boots). Nearly half the jacket is blotted with Johann's blood. Gabor wants to keep the jacket, but Mr. Budas dissuades him. How can it be cleaned? One can't take a bloodstained garment to a cleaner without the police becoming involved. Gabor relents, and Mr. Budas promises to place the jacket and boots in the casket.

We walk the muddy path to the grave site, where Gabor's parents are buried on top of each other under a white stone marker.

Mr. Budas describes how the headstone over Johann's parents' grave will be broken and refitted to include Tamas's name, if we approve. It seems odd to be asked to approve something so personal, but I nod anyway. Gabor seems eager for Ethan and me to approve everything.

Back at Mr. Budas's office, Gabor selects a wooden cross to stand as a temporary marker until the stone is ready. Then we discuss the inscription for the headstone, including the usual: name, dates of birth and death. Ethan surprises me by removing a folded page from his jacket, on which he has recorded a long poem. He suggests carving the poem's closing lines onto the stone and reads them aloud, with Kitty translating:

"We will miss you as a child misses its mother
And as brothers miss one another."

I can do nothing but nod, and everyone follows suit. Gabor adds a request, speaking directly to Mr. Budas. Kitty covers her face and—against my better judgment—I insist on knowing what Gabor has said. Kitty tells me, "Gabor asked Mr. Budas to be sure to leave room on the stone for *his* name, as he will be buried, someday, with his brother." I am incapacitated with grief, and I feel someone leading me to a car. It is Gabor—Kitty's lanky boyfriend, the black marketeer with a movie star's smile.

We return to the Hotel Bodrog and secure a room for Johann's brother. I suspect he has never stayed in a hotel before, as he doesn't seem to know what to do with his room; he stands just inside the door. Through Kitty, Ethan and I explain that we'll join him for dinner but for now we'd like to rest. When I close the door of my room, a few steps away, Gabor stands in the corridor, watching me.

The following day is filled with errands and adventures. We order flowers and buy Gabor a suit and a knee-length topcoat. We find ways to communicate when Kitty isn't around. Nodding one's head thoughtfully while saying "Ah" indicates approval. Shaking one's head vigorously while saying "Nem" (the Hungarian negative) is a veto. I veto cigarettes, and Ethan vetoes an arrangement of salmon-pink gladiolas. Gabor vetoes one of my protein bars while approving—emphatically, I gather, for our amusement—every full-breasted girl who saunters by. Ethan, smoking Hungarian cigarettes, joins in, winking at girls when Gabor points them out and once, to my amazement, pretending to cup a pair of breasts, purring, "Ah, ah."

"What are you?" I chide. "A member of the Rat Pack?"

"What do you want to do? Tell Gabor his brother was gay? Because that's the same thing. If he figures out that *we're* gay…"

"I have a feeling he figured that out back in the flower shop, when you canceled the gladiolas because they were 'too vibrant for a funeral.'"

Ethan looks stricken, as if it has never occurred to him that he does not appear—at all times, in every situation—thoroughly heterosexual.

Gabor distracts us, pointing to a nearby office building and repeating his mother's name. Ethan and I forget our argument, flummoxed by the long, excited story Gabor tells in Hungarian. He seems to have forgotten that we cannot understand him; he repeats key words, which, of course, is no help whatsoever. We are relieved when Kitty arrives. She explains that Gabor's mother used to work in the building across the street.

"That's where she had her dentist's office?" I ask.

Kitty poses the question to Gabor and translates his puzzled response: Gabor's mother was not a dentist. She was a secretary for a politician.

I'm stunned. Johann spoke often of his mother's being a dentist, of the way in which she cared for his teeth, of his discomfort with another dentist touching them. I remember him saying, "I know it sounds stupid, Ronnie, but I can't bear for another dentist to fix my teeth. I'm afraid it will make my mother in heaven jealous." I'm not surprised to have uncovered one of Johann's lies; after all, if you don't know someone's true name, what do you know about him? But this lie seems elaborate and unnecessary. What purpose does it serve to convince strangers that your mother was a dentist?

I remain puzzled by this discovery until I learn—later, at dinner—that Johann's father had been a car mechanic and not, as Johann claimed, an engineer. I see Johann had been upgrading his pedigree, from the working to middle class. A refugee from the Communist bloc, an aspiring entrepreneur who craved crème caramel, Johann was elitist.

We meet Gabor's priest in his office. Ethan has definite ideas about the funeral service, while I have none, so I cool my heels during negotiations. Ethan and the priest come to loggerheads over the number of candles to be placed about the sanctuary. Ethan suggests a hundred. I watch the father's eyes widen. He is a middle-aged man, bearded, with a heavy build; he is not unfriendly but, I sense, unused to being micromanaged. Kitty translates his response to Ethan's request for a hundred candles: "He says they usually have five."

Ethan holds to a hundred. He smiles, I smile, the priest smiles, Kitty stares at the floor, and Gabor jumps into the fray with a speech, poking the air with a pointed finger. Kitty does not translate Gabor's lecture but only the priest's curt response. "Okay. One hundred. Because you've come so far."

The grandmotherly church organist, however, cannot be persuaded to play the piece by Handel that Ethan has chosen, unfurling sheet music from his briefcase. She glances at the music, smiling but clearly bamboozled; I sense she hasn't attempted a new selection in many years. She protests that no one could learn such a complicated piece in 24 hours, and besides, it involves a choir. Who can organize a choir at such short notice?

These arguments seem reasonable to me, but Ethan claims the piece is simple enough. He stands beside her, humming a few bars and guiding his finger along the notes. Through Kitty, the organist suggests that Ethan play it himself. It is not a friendly suggestion.

I take him aside. "Look, Ethan. You might have to let this one go."

I suppose there are moments in each man's life when everything important boils down to one thing that seems unimportant to everyone else. Ethan offers no good argument, only a plea: "I *have* to hear this piece tomorrow. I can't explain it. If I don't, everything will be a waste. Not just this trip, but my time with Johann. Everything we had…wasted."

Once again I find myself crying in front of disconcerted Hungarians. "You'll hear this music tomorrow. I promise. If I have to, I'll play the fucking thing myself."

Ethan's tears are falling as well, but he chortles. "Do you play the organ?"

"Oh, Ethan," I say, trying to imitate one of Johann's lascivious smiles, "there's a wonderful answer to that question, but this isn't the place for it."

Kitty has an inspiration. She takes us to the middle school, just entering its final period, to meet Eva, the music instructor. Eva is nothing like the ample, foggy-eyed organist. Everything about Eva is sharpened: her posture, slender limbs, narrow, long fingers. She studies the Handel with skepticism, thoroughly unfazed and certainly not intimidated by our motley crew. She orders students entering the classroom to get busy at some activity while commandeering the piano to sight-read a few measures. Eva is all musician. She sings to herself. Ethan says she has the voice of an angel, and Eva rolls her eyes, no sucker for flattery. An extended interrogatory develops between Kitty and Eva while Gabor leads me to a particular desk, points to it, and says his name. I gather he has been a student at this site. I inquire, "Tommy?" meaning, "Was your brother a student here as well?" Gabor nods, saying,

"Egan, Egan," the Hungarian word for "yes." We have broken the language barrier.

Kitty summarizes her conversation with Eva. "I explained everything about Tamas and the funeral, but she can't understand why you are here. Why are two Americans doing all this for a boy from this town?"

I echo Ethan's simple answer: "He was our friend."

Our response doesn't satisfy Eva, at least not immediately. She looks into Ethan's eyes and then mine. She is young and smartly dressed, and I suspect she's putting everything together, reading the proper meaning into Ethan's use of the word "friend." With the sheet music in hand, she asks another question through Kitty: Do we expect the choir as well to be organized and ready to perform in—she checks her wristwatch—18 hours?

Ethan—the man who refused salmon-pink gladiolas and insisted upon one hundred candles—does not retreat. "Without the choir," he offers, "what's the point?"

Eva answers, "It will be done."

After dinner, in the hotel, I'm writing Johann a letter to be placed into his casket, a dramatic mea culpa, when Ethan visits. He's drinking and seems nervous and finally gets to the point: He's ready to hear the specifics of Johann's last hours. I've dreaded this task, but once I begin, the story pours forth, a tremendous release. I expect Ethan's condemnation—perhaps I crave it—and for a prompt I show him my chest, where I've carved Johann's name.

Ethan rejects the notion that I'm responsible for Johann's death. "When should you have changed your behavior to alter these events? When you met Johann? When you developed a drug problem? How many of these things do you think are in your control?"

I sense the truth of Ethan's argument. I don't own Johann, neither in life nor death. We orbited each other, we collided, but we never merged. I can claim only the qualities I projected onto Johann, what I needed him to be. I wrote a character; he played it well. It was, after all, what he did for a living.

I ask Ethan's permission to place my goodbye letter in Johann's casket. I don't know why I've assigned this authority to Ethan, but I have. Ethan leads me to his room. He shows me two greeting cards, for Valentine's Day, three weeks away. "I bought one for each of us," he explains. "Why don't you choose the one you like and put your letter inside?"

I'm so stunned by the generosity of this gesture that I require clarification. "You mean, you bought one for me, to give to Johann...before you even knew me?"

"Sure. Which one do you want?"

One card is meant for lovers, in red satin with romantic script, and I leave it for Ethan. For my goodbye to Johann, I choose a card with block letters and no inscription, suitable for an exchange between friends.

The day of Johann's burial blurs by; I abuse the anti-anxiety medication Dr. Yu prescribed for my trip. The church seems ablaze at mass, and Eva's organ and choir sound celestial; I feel as if I'm straddling this world and the next.

Ethan and I flank Gabor all day. We march through mud from the funeral chapel to the grave site, and I receive another shock: Ethan has ordered five hundred roses from Holland, in yellow, lavender, and pink, which surround Johann's grave. The locals are stunned; some of them look away, embarrassed. Bouquets of fifty roses each are tied with satin ribbons with Ethan's name, Gabor's, and mine.

"I want to help you pay for all this," I stammer.

Ethan answers, "I accept."

Johann's godmother breaks down as Johann is lowered into his grave. "I held him in my arms," she cries, "when he was a baby." Ethan and I exchange looks. Is he thinking what I'm thinking, that I held him in my arms too?

Ethan and I take Gabor to Budapest for a holiday, accompanied by Kitty and her boyfriend. We catch up with the Playboys and have to sort out the three Gabors. We call Johann's brother "Little Gabor." We refer to Kitty's boyfriend as "Kitty's Gabor," although Ethan and I—in private—name him "the Stud Muffin." Johann's former roommate, the Playboy, becomes "New York Gabor" or, sometimes, "Cio-Cio Gabor." "Cio-Cio-San" has been shortened to "Cio-Cio" and stands for several things: hello, goodbye, and mostly, "crazy."

I will not speak to Cio-Cio Gabor. He missed Johann's funeral. He claims to have fallen asleep on a train, but I'm sure he is lying. The Playboys are washed out, hungover, and Zsolt mumbles something about an orgy at a club called Caligula.

Little Gabor is fascinated by the Playboys. He can't stop quizzing them about Club Caligula, and the result is that the boys are taking him out Saturday night. Ethan and I decline an invitation to join them, and Kitty declines on her Gabor's behalf. I extract a promise from Zsolt and Cio-Cio Gabor to take care of Little Gabor, to allow nothing bad to happen to him. I threaten to murder them if they break this promise. I'm not joking.

Friday, Ethan and I drag Little Gabor to churches and museums. He spends most of his time looking at girls. Kitty has returned home, and we are left to communicate with finger-pointing and saying "Cio-Cio" in just about every situation. At lunch I draft an English-speaking waiter to ask Little Gabor if there's a particular monument or attraction he'd like to visit. The waiter quizzes Gabor and responds, "He says he would enjoy a pinball arcade."

Saturday comes and the Playboys let us down again. They are too hungover from Friday night's orgy to go out. Ethan and I are left high and dry when Little Gabor knocks on our door, expecting to meet Zsolt and Cio-Cio Gabor. He is freshly shaved, showered, sodden with hair gel, and reeking of cologne.

I say to Ethan: "I feel like it's prom night and our little boy has no date."

Ethan and I decide—insanely—that Little Gabor cannot miss his boys' night out. We dress, we gel our hair, we apply cologne. Little Gabor cannot stop giggling. He keeps cupping his hands in front of imaginary breasts, chanting, "Cio-Cio Ron, Cio-Cio Ethan, Cio-Cio Gabor."

After dinner at Burger King, Ethan and I are faced with the problem of finding a strip club. The Playboys do not answer repeated calls to their cell phones. "I hope they're dead," I say.

We enter the lobby of a tourist hotel. Ethan approaches the concierge, who speaks English. "Do you know where there's a place where, um, men can go and, um, look at women who, um, take off their clothes?"

The concierge—obviously a man of the world—points to the door. "Club Aphrodite. Right across the street."

We find Club Aphrodite across the street and wonder how we missed it in the first place; after all, there are near-naked, live women squirming to disco music in the store-front windows.

We enter, greeted by bodyguards built like professional wrestlers and find seats at the bar, which serves as a runway for the strip show. For two hours we watch indifferent strippers. Rather, we watch Gabor watch them. Girls sit beside us, and I buy everyone rounds of the house special drink, which involves champagne and cherries. At one point I catch Ethan staring lustfully at a handsome German tourist. I whisper, "Don't you think you ought to spend more time looking at the strippers and less time cruising the clients?" A sweet girl—the prettiest and youngest of the bunch—attaches herself to Gabor, and he beams. At least we've accomplished something.

When we're ready to leave, I'm presented with a bill for an enormous amount of Hungarian forints, which, when calculated, comes to fifteen hundred American dollars. The bodybuilding bouncers block the door while the manager explains that each house "special" drink costs thirty dollars, and each ten minutes a girl spends sitting on a stool, next to a customer, is considered a fifty-dollar "date." I pay the bill with my credit card.

Gabor falls asleep in the taxi between me and Ethan. His head rests on Ethan's shoulder, and drool gathers at the corner of his mouth. I'm smiling, and Ethan asks why.

"Our trip to Hungary ends with us getting scammed in a whorehouse. Don't you think that's funny?"

Ethan and I haven't spoken of Johann's profession; as far as I know, Ethan believes Johann made his living as a personal trainer. Perhaps he didn't pay Johann for sex. Perhaps they dated, as normal people date, and Ethan showered Johann with gifts, imitating relationships from closeted times, when a professional man referred to his young companion as "my protégé."

"What do you consider being scammed?" Ethan asks.

"Scammed is being lied to, when something isn't real. Ethan…" The damp streets of Budapest, viewed in the window past Ethan's head, are empty. "I don't know if anything between me and Johann was real. Was it? Between the two of you? Was it real?"

Ethan digs into his pocket for a tissue, to wipe saliva that dribbles from Gabor's lips to his chin. "What's real?" he asks. "And by the way, do you have *any* idea where this taxi is taking us?"

I don't recognize anything out the windows, not the dim movie theaters or the shuttered pastry shops.

"I don't know where we are. I don't have a fucking clue."

"Do you think we should wake Gabor to translate?"

I start to laugh.

"What's so funny?"

"He *can't* translate, Ethan. He doesn't speak English, remember?"

I laugh again and Ethan joins me, although we try not to disturb the young man sleeping between us. Ethan's arm is stretched behind Gabor, cradling him, and his hand brushes my shoulder. We are touching, if only coincidentally, and I hope Ethan doesn't move his arm and Gabor remains asleep, that we stay like this until the end of the ride, whenever the end comes, wherever it leads.

Epilogue

I haven't abused alcohol or drugs for many years. I'm no longer oppressed by urges toward self-destruction (well, no more than the average person); I never wrap belts around my neck or bang my head against a wall. In the parlance of spiritual programs, I am not cured, but I am recovering. Still, I can be obsessive (at this writing I'm training to run a marathon), but my energies are directed toward generally positive, socially responsible outcomes. This way of life is not a capitulation. It is an adventure, often confounding, sometimes joyful, but never boring.

Last year my father broke his neck (falling in a hospital room), wore a halo bolted into his skull for six months to stabilize his spine, recovered from that injury, but succumbed to pulmonary and cardiac disease and died in my arms. I kissed his face repeatedly and stroked his unshaven cheek. I like to say, when people inquire about the event, that I kissed my father into heaven.

My mother's worst nightmare came true when we placed her in a nursing home. She passes her days slumped in a wheelchair, staring at her hands. She no longer speaks and barely makes eye contact. I visit her frequently. My love for her is potent. When I feed her, wipe her nose, or clip hairs from her chin, I feel toward her as I imagine parents feel toward newborns; the boundaries of her being and mine seem porous, as if we have become—as we were once—the same person.

My brother and I have tried to reconcile but struggle to sustain a relationship. Sooner or later, a minor reason for

235

disagreement prompts an overwrought explosion. I know he is a loving husband and father, a respected friend and employer. Perhaps it's only with me that he's reminded of something from the past that stretches his patience and stirs a sleeping demon. Who knows? A week before my father died, my brother and I stood on either side of my father's hospital bed rubbing his back, and once my brother's hand brushed mine.

I fear I will offend some members of my family by telling the truth of our history, but I haven't told the entire truth. Most of my cousins, aunts, and uncles are compassionate, hardworking people. It's not my intention to besmirch our family or belittle my ancestors but to trace the alcoholism and mental illness that passed from some of them to me.

I think of Johann frequently, always on his birthday and especially at New Year's Eve. (I'm not comfortable on December 31; I don't attend parties or raise a glass at midnight.) Sometimes Johann intrudes into my thoughts out of context, a surprise guest. Once on a winter evening I struck a deer while driving. It collapsed at the side of the road. I knelt beside it, tearing up, thinking of Johann's death on a Las Vegas freeway, thinking of a miniature deer licking crème caramel from his finger at a seaside restaurant near Key West. I stroked the deer's head and asked to be forgiven. Eventually the deer rose and shook off its injury, leaping into the woods. The next day I called Johann's brother, Gabor. Our conversation was translated by Olga, the AT&T translator who assisted when Johann died and has become a part of our lives. I learned from Gabor that his brother's name day (the day on the Roman Catholic calendar dedicated to Saint Thomas) had just passed; it had, in fact, fallen on the day I'd struck the deer. When one lives in Woodstock, this kind of coincidence is taken seriously.

I no longer wrestle with questions about Johann's feelings for me. I have no questions regarding my feelings for him: I loved him with all my heart. It's true I didn't know him well; perhaps I loved a chimera and now I love a ghost. What he felt for me remains a mystery. Now and then I peruse the artifacts of our friendship: photos, a restaurant menu, and a card he sent for one of my birthdays. Inside the card, he wrote:

Dear Ronnie,
Do not worry about getting old. You are handsome, you are sexy, you are smart. But the best thing about you, Ronnie—you will have me for a friend for the rest of your life.

ACKNOWLEDGMENTS

Five years ago I joined a writers group, hoping to rekindle a career as an author of prose. I had a story to tell and believed a book was the right way to tell it. At my inaugural meeting, I sobbed through a few overwritten pages. For some reason no one asked me to leave. The members of the group expressed little interest in the elements of my story that belonged to the popular "recovery memoir" genre. They were intrigued, however, by the love affair at the core of my story and particularly by the elusive object of my desire: a self-confident, Latin-quoting Hungarian gigolo. With their help, this book—a love story—came to life, and now I'd like to thank them: John Bowers, Laura Shaine Cunningham, Casey Kurtti, Nina Shengold, Scott Spencer, Rebecca Stowe, Zachary Sklar, and Mary Louise Wilson. John and Laura did extra duty as editors, and Laura extended her support to encouraging daily e-mails and frequent hot meals. Gloria Loomis and Katherine Fausset of the Watkins-Loomis Agency found a comfortable home for *Blue Days, Black Nights* at Alyson Books. I've been bolstered by the enthusiasm of Judy Wieder; perfect notes from my astute, funny editor, Angela Brown; and the friendship of Michael Rowe, Michael Thomas Ford, Sigrid Heath, Shelley Wyant, Sandi Gelles-Cole, Anne Stockwell, and Jennifer Trask.

CREDITS

Excerpt from W. Somerset Maugham's *The Painted Veil* (published by Heineman London, 1925) reprinted by permission of The Random House Group Limited.

Excerpt from Louis Lewin's *Phantastica: A Classic Survey on the Use and Abuse of Mind-Altering Plants* © 1998 reprinted by permission of Park St. Press.

Excerpt from John Hersey's *Key West Tales* (Alfred A. Knopf Inc., © 1994) reprinted by permission of Random House.

Excerpt from Wallace Stevens's "Debris of Life and Mind" (Alfred A. Knopf Inc. © 1994) reprinted by permission of Random House.

Excerpt from Hugh Johnson's *Vintage: The Story of Wine* © 1989 reprinted by permission of Mitichell Beazley UK.

Excerpt from Malcolm Lowry's *Under the Volcano* (published by Alfred A. Knopf Inc., 1984) reprinted by permission of Harper Collins.

Excerpt from Richard Hell's "The Blank Generation" © 1977 reprinted by permission of Automatic Music, Quickmix Music Inc,. and Duraflow Music Inc. (BMG).

Excerpt from Zizek Slavoj's *For They Know Not What They Do: Enjoyment as a Political Factor* © 1991 reprinted by permission of Verso UK.